Dark Victory

Dark Victory

Through Depression to Hope

Martin Israel

MOWBRAY

Mowbray
A Cassell imprint
Wellington House, 125 Strand, London WC2R 0BB
215 Park Avenue South, New York, NY 10003, USA

First published 1995
Reprinted 1996

British Library Cataloguing in Publication Data
A catalogue record for this book is available from the British Library

ISBN 0-264-67353-0

Typeset by York House Typographic Ltd
Printed and bound in Great Britain by
Biddles Ltd, Guildford and King's Lynn

Contents

Prologue   vii

1 The state of mind   1

2 Ups and downs   11

3 Body and soul   21

4 Beauty and freedom   29

5 The pain of the world   39

6 The hope that does not pale   53

7 Moods of warmth   63

8 The sense of the ridiculous   75

9 Desolation and its aftermath   89

10 Forgiveness   103

11 Awareness of mortality   121

12 The journey into truth   133

13 The confluence of darkness and light   145

14 Recognition   157

Prologue

The purpose of this book is to consider some of the many moods that are part of the human condition. At first there was to be a special emphasis on depression, but as the scheme revealed itself in greater detail to my mind, I saw that there was much more to be considered than this very common, negative state of mind. This nevertheless has remained the central axis of the book, around which many other emotional states tend to revolve. The main theme is the clarification of various mood patterns, showing that there is nothing completely valueless in our lives provided we have the courage to persist in whatever state we may find ourselves and the integrity to accept what is shown to us as a prelude to a change in our awareness of ourselves and of the world at large. Our mood is related to our bodily health, the circumstances governing our life and our relationship with other people. This relationship is not merely one of intellectual agreement or even emotional compatibility; we also receive more immediate information from a soul communicating directly with its neighbour. There is also the direct interplay of the energies of God with those who have a mystical openness to states of being hardly known to most other people. When we can get to know the inner manifestations of various patterns of personal emotion, we can use our lives more creatively. To be able to transcend the apparently insurmountable barriers of mortality, to lose ourselves in loving service as a prelude to the unitive consciousness of the mystic is an excellent way. Yet no one should spurn the experience of depression as a way to understanding other people more compassionately. Every mood has something to offer the sensitive person; all moods are stepping-stones to an awareness of the totality of life and of our place in eternity.

1 The state of mind

Our state of mind, or mood, is governed by our emotional response at any one time. Sometimes we feel remarkably well, on top of the world, so that nothing seems beyond our capacity. Our attitude to those around us is joyful and duties that are usually rather irksome are discharged in a trice. This pleasant state of affairs is often the result of some pleasant outside circumstance, such as hearing good news. If we continue in this state indefinitely, we move into an ebullient elation. Pleasant as it may be for us personally, our hyperactivity and loquacity may become increasingly irritating to those around us, especially if our actions show an alarming disregard for our own worldly security. We may buy unnecessary articles of furniture or clothing to the extent of impoverishing ourselves, so that when we return to our senses we may find ourselves in sore financial straits. This is the state of hypomania; such a person is mentally ill and requires urgent psychiatric treatment. If not, the condition may soon proceed to mania in which patients lose all contact with reality, at the same time wearing themselves out in ceaseless, often destructive activity frequently accompanied by insulting language to those around them. If treatment is not speedily forthcoming the patient's life itself may be endangered as a result of foolhardy actions, or else he or she may succumb in a state of exhaustion. From all this we can see that the normal state of mind is finely balanced, and an excess of one type of emotion causes rapid mental disturbance.

The opposite emotional polarity shows itself in dejection, irritation and anger. We all have experienced this 'bad mood' often enough. If we are people of a relatively normal state of mind, this negative reaction will follow some irksome or unpleasant circumstance. This may be bad news, a deeply felt disappointment following the failure of a dearly regarded plan or personal relationship, or the irremediable loss of someone dear to us. This last is the universal experience of bereavement, which may include premature retirement (and also normal retirement) from previously fulfilling work as well as marital separation or the death of someone who had previously shared our lives. A bad mood may also accompany physical ill health of a temporary nature during the early period of its development. The unhappy state of mind in all these examples tends to right itself with the passage of time, though none of these misfortunes (apart from acute illness) can be rapidly expunged from our consciousness. This applies especially to the bereavement situation, which may take a full two years for complete recovery in the case of an adult's death (recovery is never complete when a child has died). But even here the mourner learns to cope with the tragedy, helped if necessary by a bereavement counsellor, so that a reasonably efficient return to work may be effected at quite an early stage in the 'work of grief', as Freud called it.

Sometimes there may be a persistent state of despondency without an obvious cause in the person's life. Alternatively the despondency may have been triggered off by one of the factors already mentioned, but a return to normal functioning simply fails to occur. Sometimes the precipitating factor is an injury, a surgical operation or a more recent successfully completed pregnancy. It would seem that once the mind is cleared of some major preoccupation, it lapses into a negative emotional state and its worst excesses of self-denigration culminating in self-destruction. This is called depression, and it is an alarmingly common mental disorder. It is a disease at least as serious as mania, for unless treated expeditiously it may terminate in a suicide attempt. Indeed, most apparently motiveless suicides have a depressive background. In some people there is such an emotional imbalance, or lability, that periods of depression and hypomania may alternate. This is called manic-depressive psychosis, or to be more learned, a 'bipolar affective disorder'. The word 'affect' means feeling or emotion, and the bipolarity refers to the nature of the disorder veering between the two polarities of mania and depression. In others with disorders of mood it is the depressive element that alone shows itself. Some types of depression run an indolently chronic course in which the person simply has no impetus to do anything except attend to the bare functions of bodily existence, whereas other depressions have an acute onset and the patient moves rapidly into a suicidal situation if not treated forthwith by a psychiatrist or general medical practitioner administering appropriate therapy; all these conditions may be called 'clinical depression'. Many of the latter group require admission to hospital, but milder cases can be treated as out-patients.

What does it feel like to be depressed? Here I can cite my own experience, one that followed a severe shoulder injury ten years ago. I had already made the mistake of being available to far too many visitors. These came ostensibly to cheer me up and support me, but in fact they often used the time for counselling, thus simply using me as they often did in my own flat. A patient in hospital is a sitting target for any commiserating visitor who deposits their problems, and more importantly their emotional, psychic debris, on to the psyche of the one who lies helpless in bed. In addition, some like myself have a depressive tendency, albeit often unrecognized. And so some of my visitors spent up to an hour with me in the afternoon, when I would have been far more profitably at rest, possibly with a light book to read or some pleasant music to hear. I have no doubt that all these people had the best intentions; they bore my injury and subsequent operation fully to heart, and some gave me beautiful flowers and potted plants, but they could not give me any peace. Towards the end of the week in hospital, the nursing staff grew aware of the situation, and saw to it that the visitors stayed for only a short time. In fact no visitor should stay for more than ten minutes, and he or she should be in a good mood before arriving, also remembering to practise periods of unobtrusive silence. To be sure, intimate family will stay longer than this, but the principle of good tidings and quietness holds good.

For the last few nights before my departure I found that I could not fall asleep after I had woken up in the middle of the night, and the nursing staff gave me tablets for pain; these soon sent me to sleep again, and I did not understand the import of what was happening. Then came the time of discharge. As I left the hospital with a friend, I nearly burst into tears as I said 'Now I can see what a selfish life I have been leading; I am thoroughly ashamed of myself. Now my eyes are open to the self-centred existence I enjoy.' This was to say the least a very hard judgement on my life-style. Certainly all of us who live alone are in danger of being selfish and careless of the needs of other people, but the condemnation could not in truth be applied to me. When I had completed my medical lecturing and the care of my church with its various services, I spent most evenings up to 10 p.m. being available for a counselling and healing ministry. The criticism of my way of life was, and even now to a considerable extent still is, that I did far too much work and did not give myself an adequate break. But what can one do when so many people require assistance? What I demonstrated was a classical symptom of depression: a drastic lowering of self-esteem. Self-esteem is not to be confused with egoistic pride or narcissism, both of which tend to boost the personality to unreal heights. Self-esteem simply accepts the value of oneself as a person as part of the great mass of humanity in which one works and to which one bestows one's particular gift. If one lacks self-esteem, one cannot contribute properly to the social milieu: one feels one is quite useless to the point that one's absence or even death would occasion little loss to those around one.

When I left the hospital I was taken care of by a devoted parishioner, an elderly widow with whom I had a close spiritual rapport. The condition of my shoulder would have precluded living alone for some weeks or even months. But the even greater problem was the mounting depression. I was despondent, secretly tearful, and filled with doubts about the eventual recovery of the shoulder – a not entirely irrational fear, since there had been a reprehensible delay in operating on the joint. The physiotherapist was excellent, but the axillary nerve damage seemed, fortunately wrongly, to be permanent. Furthermore he was due to leave soon for some other country with his girl-friend, and I doubted whether his replacement would be nearly as efficient as he. Once again my fears proved wrong. The main suffering, however, was the intractable insomnia which had already showed itself while I was in hospital. I could fall asleep easily enough, but once I had awoken there was little possibility of any further sleep. The time of awakening could vary – anything from 5 a.m. to 1 a.m. – it is no joke to lie awake from the earliest hours of the morning to about 7 a.m., when the household begins its normal day. In a state of depression even well-loved books lose their savour, and so there is no question of reading oneself back to a pleasant fatigue which culminates in dropping off to sleep once more. In fact the insomnia of depression is often accompanied by fatigue but there is small chance of any ensuing sleep. Music likewise loses its inspirational quality and tends to pall in the ears, as does even the choicest food on the taste buds of the tongue.

I also was abnormally anxious; when my hostess went out early in the evening to visit friends I was in quite a state of agitation, as if the house might be entered into and burgled during her absence. When she returned I heaved a sigh of inner relief. I have pondered on the apparent foolishness of this reaction: even if I had felt quite ill, I would have been loath to disturb my elderly benefactor. And, in any case, what could she have done other than summon the doctor, an action I was quite capable of performing on my own? It seems that her immediate presence provided a support for my delicately exposed soul. Some people emit a negative psychic emanation which tends to repel sensitive individuals, whereas others are surrounded by a positive psychic force, or strength, and affection which supports anyone with poor self-esteem and personal anxiety, so that they can survive in the knowledge that at least someone really cares for them to the extent of giving themself to his or her well-being. This is a crucial test of love, that a person who cares will stop at nothing to protect and heal the other creature.

I soon consulted the general practitioner who looked after me, and he gave me a very effective antidepressant tablet that settled the insomnia within a single night. My mood swung back to something of its wonted positive response to life rather more slowly, but the relief from the sleeplessness itself gave me a more optimistic view of events, including my shoulder injury. I co-operated with the physiotherapist even more unceasingly than before, but I still had to wait several months for the injured nerve to start a repair process sufficient for me to lift the arm into the air when I was lying on a couch. And so I learned valuable lessons in faith, patience and courage.

As I convalesced from the combined effects of the surgical operation and the depression, two symptoms showed themselves. There was first an undue emotional response to music of the Romantic period: I could scarcely stop myself weeping when familiar pieces of Schumann and Mendelssohn were broadcast over the radio; such a response was quite foreign to my hearing any music, great music lover that I am. The music seemed to clear my memory of much contemporary material and lay it open to events that had occurred many years previously when I was a mere youth. It took about a week for this heightened emotional sensitivity to resolve into a normal reaction to musical stimulation.

The second symptom was again something quite foreign to me previously: a fear of enclosed places. This showed itself when I was travelling in a moderately filled London underground train. The line on which I was travelling lay close to the surface, but the train was delayed for several minutes in a tunnel. My agitation mounted almost to fever pitch; although I could see quite clearly that this reaction was unnecessary, I still could scarcely control my anxiety, which was one of dying in the tunnel. This was quite out of keeping with my usual response to death, which I had seen as a welcome phenomenon once one's work was completed in the world. Now my basic fear was unmasked despite my intellectual attitude. There was also a morbid fear of being trapped in an enclosed space, the familiar state of claustrophobia. This had never so much as occurred to me as a possibility until then. Several weeks later I was once again delayed in an underground train, this time on a line deeply under the surface, but then my reactions were quite normal.

Despite this recital of the travail of clinical depression, I have purposely omitted the most terrible feature: a feeling of being sucked into oneself where there is no one to acknowledge, let alone receive, one's existence. In other words, as far as language can describe personal feelings, I was being drawn, almost sucked, into a state of hell, where there was intolerable emotional pain emanating from the centre of the body, especially the abdominal area. The pain had a dull physical quality, and was accompanied by a sensation of utter desolation and mounting fear. I had experienced this before in moments of worry and tension, but it soon wore off. In my depression it lingered, mounting in intensity in paroxysms of hopelessness. In my present situation, in which activity was severely curtailed, I had no way of allaying the terrible suffering. I have little doubt that this 'emotional pain' is the feature of severe depression that tempts its victims with the apparently blissful oblivion of suicide. For even if the punishments for vice promised by traditional religion are carried out, they pale into a gentle hue when compared with the living hell of clinical depression.

There are all varieties and stages of depression from the acute illness I have already described that responds rapidly to standard antidepressant therapy to the chronic state of hopelessness which is often accompanied by somnolence rather than insomnia. Such a person has no desire, let alone will, to do anything despite their gifts, sometimes in a number of capacities. Suicide may be threatened, but is not often carried out; it would seem as if the victim does not even possess the power to execute this resolve. Instead they remain a lasting burden on their family, whose patience is almost beyond praise; it is evident that love, sometimes hidden among the welter of destructive emotions which the incapacity of the victim evokes, remains triumphant, usually strengthened by the hope of eventual recovery. The most terrible type of depression is one in which the clinical state I described earlier simply does not respond to conventional drugs. Electro-convulsive therapy, usually shortened to ECT, sometimes works wonders in these people – an electric current is passed directly through the brain of a properly sedated patient. There may be a dramatic return to normality, nowadays with little change in the personality (this treatment is especially useful in elderly victims of depression), but sometimes this manoeuvre has no effect. Some of these cases alternate rapidly between depression and mania with only short lucid periods between them, while others remain persistently depressed with only slight periods of amelioration. The suffering here is cruel. Psychotherapy, which is frequently practised in cases of depression, finds its greatest value during periods of relative lucidity; with those in the throes of the disorder, communicative silence is by far the kindest way to approach the person.

These sombre considerations bring us to the tragic act of committing suicide. All the great world religions are at one in proclaiming the sanctity of life. Life is God's greatest gift to us; the atheist would prefer to use such a term as the 'creative principle of existence' in place of the personal God of theistic religion, but there would still be a great concern for the quality of individual life. Can one dare to throw God's greatest gift to us in his face? But is life always a great gift? When one considers the great army of individuals with diseases that have been inherited, or abnormalities they have sustained at or before birth, one can hardly avoid questioning the competence, even the love, of the Creator. St Paul wrestles somewhat superficially with the problem in Romans 9.14–21, and comes to the conclusion that God is free to do what he wants with his creatures. I think there may be a greater truth here than even Paul envisaged. In a vast scheme that goes far beyond the urgent call of the present time, it is possible that we are growing into finer, more loving people. Vicissitudes play an important part in this process of growth. In this case the present hell on earth is preparing us for a caring role in the future, whether in this present life or in some posthumous existence. The story of Job's trials, their cause and their triumphant conclusion, seem to give some substance to this conjecture. I do not accept a punitive God who visits suffering on his creatures when they anger him. His nature is always merciful, but in order for us to attain truly adult stature we have to undergo various trials. If we are zealous in our prayers, we are always close to the Deity, who sustains us in our extremity. This view is helpful in those with a clear mind, but can it take in the mentally ill also? Here lies the mystery. I believe that if those afflicted with mental disease have practised prayer before their present condition struck, they will be sustained during their ordeal. This was, I am convinced, a saving factor in my own illness. Not only had I practised intercessory prayer for many years previously, but I also did not cease praying, very inadequately, when I was ill. This served in addition to lift my mind from my own pain to the sufferings of so many people I knew personally and to the world generally. In addition, the mentally ill need our intercessions at all times and in all places.

It seems to me that suicide does not help; the problem remains on the other side of death, and it demands a proper conclusion. This is why I discourage the self-destructive act unless it forms the basis of frank martyrdom in unspeakably vile circumstances. But here we have to make up our own minds, remembering the statement of Romans 12.19, 'Vengeance is mine, says the Lord, I will repay'. It is very easy to pass judgement as an uninvolved bystander, but when we ourselves are personally involved, whether as a near relative or a sufferer, we see things from a different perspective. A last thought: it may be commendably brave to face death calmly, but even more courageous is it to face life, a life whose quality has been tragically diminished by a bodily or mental affliction, insufficient to cause death but sufficient to deprive one of the joys that make living worthwhile. When one sees the blind, the deaf, the paralysed and the chronically mentally ill going about their business as best they can, one is filled with a compassion that steadily expands into admiration and silent homage. They have made the grade: they at least show the fibre of human excellence. It remains to be seen whether we will pass the test in our own time.

2 Ups and downs

Most of us have our periods of good humour and bad temper, and these are separated by long stretches of quiet contentment in which we do our work efficiently and in harmony with those around us. Contentment can easily degenerate into complacency when we sincerely believe that all is right with the world and with us by inclusion. Such a selfish view of existence has little sympathy, indeed understanding, for those of our brethren who cannot live up to the model of success that we have erected for ourselves. It is therefore beneficial that we are periodically cut down to size by less successful episodes, success in this superficial evaluation being a state in which we enjoy the world's prizes without consideration of our own moral well-being. Let me say at once that worldly success is not to be summarily dismissed, even deprecated, for it should be the result of clean, sober, morally immaculate living. The Parable of the Talents in Matthew 25.14–30 stresses that we are expected to use the gifts with which we have been endowed to the benefit of a Master who in the first case gave them to us. This Master can be identified with the Creator whom we may call God, who in turn would expect us to use these talents to the benefit of our fellow creatures, according to the following parable, Matthew 25.31–46. Here Christ is identified with the diseased and fallen creatures languishing on the wayside of a dynamic life frequented by a busy population too intent on its own interests to notice anyone else on the way. From all this we can distinguish a false success from a true one. The first is self-centred to the extent of using all creatures on the way for its own benefit – or what it mistakenly regards as its benefit. True success leads to the growth of the person into an integrity that mirrors the great saints of humanity, and this growth into sanctity spreads far beyond the limits of the individual personality to influence vast populations of humans hovering indecisively between good and evil, between life and death.

It is a moment of trauma to be conceived in the maternal womb and to grow from the solitary zygote into an embryo whose differentiation into organs and external features is so rapid and at the same time so co-ordinated that a person begins to take shape almost under our very eyes. There is a school of psychotherapeutic thought that stresses the importance of the emotional state of the mother in initiating the mental conditioning of the foetus. However this may be, the foetus is soon born, and is then confronted with a combination of undemanding maternal love and cruelty of some kind or other by adults who are emotionally disturbed. Child abuse has recently become a burning issue as if it were a new phenomenon, but in fact it is as old as human nature. In most instances it shows itself purely in physical cruelty, but in more than a few there is also sexual interference with the unfortunate, defenceless child. I remember vividly how a very fat attendant, called a 'nurse', belaboured me with blows and abuse when I was four years old. I suspect that her evil actions were motivated by an amalgam of jealousy that I was so well-proportioned and good-looking and unassimilated regret that she could never have a child of her own. Being an only child, a truly mixed blessing or curse depending on how one regards the matter, I had no contemporary peer either to share my suffering or to offer support. My parents seemed tragically oblivious of all the suffering rained down upon me. At one time I believed I was especially unfortunate, but my later work in the counselling field taught me how mild my pain had been in comparison with that of many other people.

One thing is certain, the suffering and my exposed situation as an only child had a permanent effect on my psychological development. I became withdrawn and unable to cope with the company of other children. I felt greatly inferior to them, so much so that if anyone had praise for me, I glowed and expanded to almost magical proportions. The poor self-esteem that seems to form the basis of the depressive type of personality was inculcated early in my development. In fact I suffered from minor episodes of depressive illness long before the major eruption that I described in the last chapter, but these were so well overlaid by intellectual exhibitionism and compulsive activity that I was easily able to cope with and conceal my disability. I survived an emotionally starved childhood by spontaneously developing my intellectual faculty, thereby parrying the natural brutality of the children around me at school. This state of affairs is common enough, but is worth describing in relation to the equally common depressive state. There was, however, another factor which is less often discussed: the inner life of the person. The phrase 'inner life' occasions unease amongst many professional carers even nowadays. I remember with discomfort even today the response I produced about fifteen years ago when I attended a conference on causative elements in cancer. The usual exogenous (exterior, environmental) ones were discussed, and then I was asked to make a contribution. I said with great trepidation that we professionals should also consider the inner life of the patient. The deadly silence that ensued cowed me into a state of near-paralysis, but quite soon the wise scientific words of the conference continued. I escaped from this group as quickly as possible, my innate shyness reaching a nadir of shame (as if I had been guilty of an indecent act) as I drove home from the provincial centre. The person who had put my name forward as a potential contributor, I subsequently discovered, had completely forgotten my 'contribution' and merely said that the conference had not been a conspicuous success. I was rather relieved that my indiscretion had apparently gone largely unnoticed amongst the learned workers present at the gathering.

Our inner life includes the state of mind that our background has produced through our past experience. But there may at least in some individuals also be an awareness of a reality that is apart from the affairs of the local scene. This is the intimation of the mystic that lies embedded but largely disregarded in the depths of the psyche of a surprisingly large number of people. This awareness tells us that there is more to our mortal life than merely what confronts us in our daily encounters with the world, whether in living out various relationships with our loved ones and colleagues or in making our living by actualizing our gifts and talents amid the varied activities around us. Our gifts provide us with the recompense necessary for survival, while our relationships make that survival a meaningful effort and one of joyful recognition. 'All real living is meeting', wrote Martin Buber, the authority on a lovely type of Jewish mysticism called Hasidism that flourished in Eastern Europe in the eighteenth and nineteenth centuries, and was obliterated by the Nazism of the twentieth (except for a small remnant in Israel). It is not difficult to dismiss these transcendent stirrings as emotional compensations that the psyche evokes in order to render the present sufferings endurable, but they seem to come out of their own accord, and help to raise the person from a persistent position of complaint to one of patience and endurance with a song of joy in the heart. One somehow knows that all is well in a situation far beyond human experience, and can continue with one's work despite 'the slings and arrows of outrageous fortune' against which Hamlet inveighs in his famous soliloquy. While we live in this world there are many experiences that only some people can acknowledge; whether they are products of a diseased mind or intimations of a reality greater than is available to most of us cannot be definitively proved. But the criterion given by Jesus is the important practical one, 'You will recognize them by their fruit' (Matthew 7.16 and 20). If a person suffering the pains of mortality, whether through outer circumstances or inner torment, can still present a smiling face to the world and behave with intrepid self-control and concern for the feelings of others, that person is close to the divine source however we may choose to define that source. Human folly usually parodies wisdom most pathetically when it solemnly gives dogmatic judgements about matters of which it is blindly ignorant. This, for instance, applies to the familiar near-death experience which is written off by nearly all psychologists as merely a giant hallucination conjured up by a failing brain. Be this as it may, one can hardly dismiss the subsequent moral and spiritual effect this hallucination produces when the subject returns to normal consciousness. To quote

Hamlet once more, 'There are more things in heaven and earth, Horatio, than are dreamt of in your philosophy'.

Returning now to my own inner life, the topic which sparked off this long dissertation, I was aware even as a small child that, though the dice of happy material living was loaded against me, and, far more important, always would be loaded against me, I had important work to accomplish in this world, and that I was, and would be, supported from a much higher level than mere mundane sources. This focus of supranatural awareness I intuitively identified with God, and throughout my life, even during the severe depression I previously described, the awareness did not forsake me. But I had to strive harder to reach it; thus my prayer life continued albeit at a much lower ebb than normal. This sense of destiny did not in any way boost my ego; I have already described my low state of self-esteem which was accompanied by a paralysing shyness, which even today as a man in his later sixties is still, much less severely, with me when I move socially among strangers. But paradoxically – and spiritual modalities seem always to have a paradoxical quality – my shyness also emphasized my uniqueness, which set me apart from other people. Thus the thought of terminating my life simply did not occur to me even when I was feeling very low. On the contrary, I developed an iron will so that I might achieve those objectives for which I strove.

The will is a function of the personality that even today is often poorly understood. It is often claimed that free will is a pure illusion. We are, so it is said, merely the objects of circumstances in our environment on the one hand, and forces in our unconscious on the other. The psychic energy that poses as the will is simply being driven by one of these two sources against which we are powerless to resist. As an example, take the man whose will is to make as much money as possible: to do this he will practise parsimony in his private life while doing everything in his business to accumulate wealth. Eventually he may succeed in making his fortune, but to what end? The answer is likely to be security against misfortune, or the wish to move in esteemed social circles where show is impressive, or to ensure that his children are well educated as a preparation for a 'successful' life (the poor children are really hostages to their father's possessive-ness and the unrealized ideals in his own life). But there is in addition to this a focus in us all, though realized in only the few, which is truly ourselves; it is called the soul, or true self. This responds to the moral imperative of acting according to truth and common decency which we know as part of our own being. While this centre may be ignored or swept aside according to the convenience of the moment, its impact cannot be perpetually ignored. As Jesus puts it, 'What does anyone gain by winning the whole world at the cost of his life? What can he give to buy his life back?' (Mark 8.36–37). This life is the soul, which is the arbiter of what we really stand for. He says also 'Where your treasure is, there will your heart be also' (Matthew 6.21). When our treasures are worldly they are merely egoistical, but when a deeper chord is struck, usually as a result of misfortune that tears away the mask of illusion, the soul is laid bare, and its insistence on the higher values is obeyed. It would seem that my soul has always been in a bare state, hence my natural grasp of psychical and spiritual realities even when very young. The soul is excruciatingly vulnerable, and is as sensitive to emotional wounding as the retina of the eye is to light. The sight would be permanently destroyed if one were to look directly into the sun even for a short time, and the retina is shielded by the contraction of the iris, which makes the pupil smaller, when it is exposed to intense light. It would seem that the soul also has an inbuilt means of protection, which is its capacity to act positively against invidious stimuli, doing what it considers to be right. This action of the soul is the free will; it will disregard convention when it knows that it has to act independently. This is the way of the hero, but is not on this account automatically right. The soul itself has to be guided by the spirit within (using spatial metaphors) where the Spirit of God, the Holy Spirit, is known. It is present at that point which is both within the soul and transcends it on a universal level.

It seems to me that when one is depressed the soul is especially vulnerable. Its own will is diminished, and the superficial ego seems to be swept away by the emotional influences among which it normally plays its part in the world's affairs. The over-sensitivity of the soul is severe until it is relieved by an antidepressant drug which calms the mind, allowing precious sleep to start a healing process. I recall two incidents in my youth that demonstrate my iron will; I will recount them though neither is creditable. The first occurred in an upper form of my school. A fellow pupil wanted to borrow a book of mine, but I steadfastly refused. He was one of a group who were unfriendly to me, and I stood out against his request. The lady in charge of the class was asked by the boy to intervene and suggest that I yielded to his request and give him the book for a loan, but I remained adamant. And there the matter rested. The boy was angry and pinched me hard, but I did not care. I did not see why I should be coerced into lending my property to an unfriendly fellow pupil.

The other incident, even more reprehensible, occurred several years later when I was a medical student. I was attending a ward round directed by the professor of medicine. Suddenly there came a request from the nurses to help to turn round in bed another professor who had bone cancer, an extremely painful condition. Volunteers were requested, and the professor directing the ward round glanced in my direction, but I did not move. The dying professor was a noted racist, and I had the greatest sympathy for the black people of the country. The event occurred in South Africa some ten years before the implementation of the grossly unjust apartheid system, in which blacks were segregated in sub-standard parts of the country or in locations if their labour was required in the larger cities. Nevertheless my attitude was hard and judgemental. My will was of the Old Testament flavour with justice as its motive, rather than that of the New Testament with its emphasis on love. I subsequently embraced Christianity sufficiently to become an Anglican priest, but I have sadly to admit that the spirit of love is as far from many Christian groups as it is from non-believers and those of other religious per-suasions. It is the person who determines the sentiment of the religion just as much as the religion that influences the goodness of the person. Events in Northern Ireland and Bosnia at this present time endorse this judgement.

My will determined my life-style even as a youth. I knew I would never marry, and that a life of solitary asceticism was in store for me. I envied those who married and especially those who gave birth to children, but I had to leave these desires behind me as I forged my own way ahead. This was to embrace many years of medical practice, while subterranean forces were moving me ever closer to the Church and ordination. I did not like these movements, but I knew I had to conform, and not play the part of a ridiculous Jonah. This consideration brings us back once more to the question of free will. In fact I believe that much in our lives is predestined; we can either work with the tide by being obedient and living decent lives or else we can deliberately or unwittingly flout the rules of constructive living and fail in the mission ahead of us. I know of many gifted professional men and artists who have ruined their careers by their addiction to alcohol, promiscuous sex, or occult practices of the 'black' type. God clearly shows us the way, but does not force us to follow. His grace is abundant for all who will receive, but it needs to be accepted in the faith which finds its apogee in undemanding love. Shakespeare writes in *Julius Caesar*: 'There is a tide in the affairs of men, which, taken at the flood, leads on to fortune; omitted, all the voyage of their life is bound in shallows and in miseries.' At the end of the last chapter I mentioned the apparent arbitrary gifts of God in relation to the growth of the personality, so that some people are severely handicapped in the race of life. But it could be that these individuals are specially gifted, for if they can triumph over their adversities, they can make a greater contribution to human advancement into spiritual knowledge than masses of 'normal' people whose lives seem merely to skirt the outposts of reality as they go on from one 'success' to another. The Psalmist has much to say about the illusory prosperity of the unjust, but I suspect that the same is true of the many unimaginative types of individuals who close their eyes to reality rather like the priest and the Levite in the Parable of the Good Samaritan (Luke 10.30–37). Only when misfortune dogs their steps may they sit down and consider their lives in greater depth. 'Now come, let us argue this out, says the Lord. Though your sins are scarlet, they may yet be white as snow; though they be dyed crimson, they may become white as wool. If you are willing to obey, you will eat the best that earth yields' (Isaiah 1.18–19). But as the prophecy continues, recalcitrance will be followed by war and destruction.

3 Body and soul

The problem is perennial: is the mind a product of the brain or has it an independent existence, working through the medium of the brain while we are alive, but capable of a continuing existence once the body dies? The weight of scientific opinion is heavily drawn to the first conclusion, that mind and brain are inseparable, and that when you are dead, you certainly are dead. Nevertheless, the religious consciousness of the world is less sure, and all the major religions envisage some sort of posthumous survival of the personality without the body to direct it. The development of computers that seem to be able to do just about everything, a situation called artificial intelligence, is claimed to substantiate the materialistic position in no uncertain way. And yet many of us feel that there is something in human personality that has an autonomy denied even the most advanced computer.

The data of psychical research, or parapsychology, do seem to suggest that mind can act independently of the brain both during life and after death, but the problem lies in the unpredictability of the phenomena and the impossibility, at least at present, of reproducing them at will. The scientific view insists, quite reasonably, on the reproducibility of its data, so that these can be compared in different laboratories, their effects measured, and the whole embraced in a working theory. It is evident that the mind–brain problem cannot be solved scientifically. But there are other modalities of truth besides the scientific model. These are essentially phenomenological: we may study the phenomena as they appear, and see if any pattern of occurrence can be deduced that may give us a clue as to its significance in the lives of the people who claim to experience these effects, and by extension the lives of humans at large. If an unusual occurrence cuts across the normal flow of one's life, such as a sudden awareness of something about to happen that is proved later to have been quite accurate and could not have been anticipated beforehand (precognition), or a feeling of unease with a certain stranger or in an unfamiliar room which is later proved to be accurate, inasmuch as the person turns out to be a criminal or the room the seat of a suicide, one cannot fail to be impressed. Of course it may have been mere coincidence such as is common enough in daily living, but the import of the information makes one uneasy at this glib explanation, and if these types of phenomena recur in one's life, one feels that a deeper explanation needs to be forthcoming.

Is depression a disease of the brain or is it a reaction to unfortunate circumstances earlier on in one's life such as I mentioned in the last chapter? Speaking personally, I come down unequivocally in favour of the psychiatric view, that depression is due to cerebral dysfunction and can usually be alleviated and finally cured by antidepressant drugs. But the 'cure' concerns only a single attack, for there is a tendency for the condition to recur. In this case another course of antidepressants may lead the patient back to normality, until either the tendency ceases of its own accord or else one has to steel oneself to the label of being a 'depressive'. Some people I know who fluctuate miserably between mania and depression, such as I described in Chapter 1, tell me that they can suddenly feel something give way in their head as the wonderful period of lucidity is shattered once again by their bipolar disorder. This to me proves the essential brain disorder in severe depression with or without a maniacal component.

Sometimes an attack of depression seems to occur out of the blue, but quite often there is a clearly precipitating factor, such as a sudden disappointment or bereavement. This type of depression used to be called 'reactive', but in fact it is not essentially different from the 'endogenous' type that occurs spontaneously without any preceding cause. Whereas most of us are able to cope with these misfortunes of life after a variable period of dejection and anger, the depressive type of individual continues in a negative phase indefinitely. The basic factor may well be a peculiar type of brain dysfunction, but if the person were able more to cope with their character problems, they might not react so negatively that a brain reaction became inevitable. It is in this situation that the possible difference between brain and mind could be worth considering. This is where psychotherapy is of significance. One cause of depression is the experience of abuse during early (and sometimes later) childhood. The poor child may be defiled by sexual assault in addition to being hurt by physical violence. It cannot fight back, and even if the period of abuse ends, the child still bears its stigma. Residual depression is a valuable clue in child abuse cases. Such children continue to think poorly of themselves, and this can easily continue into adult life. Their attitude to genital sex is also frequently warped, either fearing it or else participating in a loveless promiscuity. In due course this negative attitude to life and its pleasures can culminate in an attack of clinical depression. Merely alleviating this medically is clearly insufficient, for the condition is sure to recur. Only patient psychotherapy which painstakingly broaches the cause of the trouble is likely to produce a real change in attitude. At least the cause of the problem is uncovered. In fact healing requires something in addition: a living faith that life, no matter how painful it has been, still has a deeper purpose. This is where the spiritual (a word I much prefer to religious) perspective becomes important. When one reads Viktor Frankl's moving book about his experiences in Nazi concentration camps, *Man's Search for Meaning* (London: Hodder & Stoughton, 1964), we can see how the belief in something important can keep people alive in the most gruesome circumstances. And if that something has a spiritual basis, by which I mean an objective to nobility of character and service to one's fellows, a great blessing may accrue that makes all the suffering seem worthwhile. To the materialist all this is tragic illusion, but then we are entitled to ask what his or her life has really contributed either to their growth as people or to the benefit of their fellow creatures.

Unresolved anger is another potent cause of depression. If anger, which is often a natural response to injustice of one type or another, is not satisfied, it may either flare out into destructive acts of antisocial behaviour or else eat inward to produce depression. One can imagine a person with an important message they feel they are meant to give the world. If they are disregarded or classed as mere cranks, they will feel the bitterness of impotence, and soon depression will show itself. A considerable portion of my own depression as a child was due to the fact that I was a natural mystic of high degree who was completely unable to communicate my feelings and insights with anyone in my vicinity. I am, many years later, finding that this is by no means an exceptional state of affairs. In South Africa I was virtually completely on my own; when I emigrated to Britain I gradually encountered fellow spirits, nearly all women and mostly considerably older than I. A cynic would point to their performing a maternal function in a lonely young man's life, but in fact they played no part in my day-to-day existence (I had always been very independent in my private life until the accident that precipitated the depression I described in Chapter 1, by which time I was no longer young). Women, on the whole, are more intuitive than men, and are likely to accommodate ideas that are almost beyond the masculine imagination. I have met only a very few men with whom I could have a deep conversation. My counselling work, interestingly enough, has evoked deeper thoughts in numerous men who have come to consult me.

My friend and collaborator Katherine Tetlow, whose inner life story has many points of contact with my own, and who is doing remarkable psychotherapeutic work at the present time, has suggested a scheme of inner development undergone by those who are unable to communicate their spiritual riches to their family and school peers. First there is a phase of anger, and this is followed by depression such as I have just described. If there is no relief and the person is strong-willed and of independent nature (like myself), the process proceeds to indifference and finally to a state of living one's own inner life in trust and integrity without regard to the world around one. This state she calls autism, but it is of a different quality from that of autistic children, who are generally incapable of communicating to any satisfactory degree with even their closest relatives. In what might be called 'spiritual autism' there is no difficulty in living in normal communication with the surrounding world, so that its basic demands are

24

satisfied and one earns one's living adequately by serving the community according to one's particular gifts. But in the depths of one's inner life, space is given for the experience of mystical union that renders the world's criteria of success very trivial indeed. It need hardly be said that such an autistic existence is lonely, indeed fearful, until one has come to a full acceptance of the situation and is no longer afraid to show oneself in one's entirety to society in general. I believe that such people are the forerunners of a new type of human, pioneers in fact, and as with pioneers in general, the course is rough and uncompromising with martyrdom as a possible end. It could be argued that there is really little new in all this. Surely the saints and mystics of all the religious traditions have experienced rejection until late in their lives, or after their martyred deaths. But what I am describing is a secular phenomenon. Though the types of people involved may have an allegiance to a religious tradition, their lives are not dictated by that tradition. On the contrary, they are free agents, as far as anyone can be free in this world. They can neither claim any support from a religious organization, nor would they seek it. They would rather see themselves as servants for all people irrespective of religious affiliation. Their end is the service of God as Jesus showed in his ministry. There is no account in the Gospel of Jesus interrogating anyone about their religious observance; it was their state of mind that concerned him. As I have already quoted, 'Where your treasure is, there will your heart be also' (Matthew 6.21).

From all this it would appear that depression can stem from at least two psychological roots: a loss of self-confidence and an inability to communicate one's own spiritual insights to other people, who, to quote another of Jesus' analogies, are like pigs to whom pearls are thrown. They trample on them, and then turn round and tear you to pieces (Matthew 7.6). This is why it is unwise to discuss spiritual experiences with destructively agnostic folk, and why one should seek the help of a therapist who is at least open to the possibility of spiritual reality, by which I mean the existence of God. On the other hand, a dogmatically committed believer may also be dangerous in that they can deposit their prejudices unconsciously as well as deliberately on to their client. The schools of psychotherapeutic practice are legion. Apart from the loyal followers of Freud and Jung there are the group that stress the object-relations theory of personality. Some, on the other hand, practise Gestalt therapy, others transactional analysis, others again the overtly spiritual way of psychosynthesis, and there is also cognitive therapy, which is claimed to be especially useful in depression. This examines the links between a person's thoughts and emotions, and how these affect their mental health. Quite a few are clearly cranky, and can cause bad after-effects on their unfortunate victims. There is alas no disciplinary body in psychotherapy comparable to those regulating medical, legal or accounting practice. Considering this confusing maze, one is wise to exercise caution, and above all take care not to surrender one's own inner belief system to any one school of psychotherapy any more than to a religious tradition. The basic ideas are often praiseworthy, but in the end it is the integrity of the individual therapist that matters, and here the concept of love is all-important. It is the capacity of the therapist to empathize fully with the client that is of far greater importance than the philosophy that guides his or her thoughts.

In my last term at school one of the masters asked me what I intended to do when I left; I mentioned medical study (my father was a doctor), but he suggested that I considered the practice of psychoanalysis, a word that meant little to me at that time. When I look back on my life I often wonder how I escaped some sort of psychotherapy, since I had poor self-esteem and a tendency to depression. Yet an inner wisdom, my inner voice as I call it, directed me sharply from this course of action. As an older man I can at last see the wisdom of the inner caution: I had my own unique way to traverse, indeed I had to fashion that way. The one certainty I had was the divine presence around me. How easy it would have been for a well-meaning therapist to have proved that this divine presence was merely an illusion that allowed me to escape the demands of the world around me, especially marriage and the work of the householder, as the Hindu puts it! Nothing is more gratifying than to interfere with the life-style of another person, naturally for their own good! And my own state of unhappiness would have surely justified this interference.

Fortunately for me I obeyed the inner injunction and kept on my solitary way with intrepid resolution despite my emotional pain. The result has been an outpouring of spiritual wisdom both in lecturing and in writing, quite spontaneous and inspirational, that is little short of a miracle (a word which means something to wonder at). My capacity to empathize is also the fruit of long inner experience of myself, and now a ministry of deliverance has been added to my quota of work.

I do not write all this either to boost my own ego or to denigrate the value of psychotherapy; the first is sufficiently well recognized not to require any further advertisement, while the second undoubtedly helps individuals to come more to terms with themselves. But it is a fearful thing to expose your inner life to an unfeeling person. Therefore one should be very careful to choose wisely whom to consult about this delicate matter.

I attribute the severe depression I had ten years ago to gross overwork and a bodily injury acting together on a brain especially liable to depressive dysfunction. I mentioned in Chapter 1 that I tried to combine medical lecturing, the charge of a church, and healing/counselling work up to 10 p.m. in mid-week evenings. How I survived as long as I did is a mystery. I suspect that the injury came in order to force me to review my style of living. Since then I have gradually dispensed with all medical teaching, and cut down the time of seeing people to a latest appointment of 6 p.m. Even now I realize that I am overdoing my activities, but if one has special gifts, I believe they are meant to be used for the benefit of those who need them most. If I had been married, my activities would have been centred around my family. Being unattached, I see all those who need assistance as my family, in this way following the example of Jesus (Mark 3.31–35). An extremely psychic person like me picks up negative moods from others very quickly, and I am aware of incipient depressions very soon. I have found that if I lift up the situation to God in prayer at once, the depression lifts. Then I can continue the counselling work. Fortunately only a minority of my clients 'drain' me in this way. Many more are delightful people whose company I relish. They have their domestic, occupational, or spiritual problems which we can talk over in uninhibited ease. I seldom give advice, and that only when I am asked quite specifically my opinion about the matter, but from our time together they seem to pick up the guidance of the Holy Spirit, and leave satisfied with what is to be in their future lives. The Holy Spirit works best through a mind that is clear and at ease, not trying to be right at all costs or to justify itself. When we are aware of our ignorance, we are often of most help; when we know the answer before we have heard the question fully, we are most dangerous. In other words, humility is the essence of all healing and counselling work. In that state we are completely open to the Holy Spirit and may give the word that heals. By contrast, pride and arrogance occlude the Holy Spirit from our consciousness, for then we believe we know it all, and there is nothing else that we should hear. A good therapist is a model of natural humility, not the obsequious humility of a Uriah Heep, but the open childlike attitude of one who regards every phenomenon of life, and especially every human, with a mixture of awe and joy, of courtesy and delight.

To end where we started, I believe that mind and brain are two distinct entities. While we are alive, the mind works fully through the mechanism of the brain even if it picks up information in an extra-sensory, extra-rational way. But when the body dies, I look for more experience in the after-life with a now freed mind. This is a confession of faith, not a declaration of knowledge. As Jesus says, 'Do not be anxious about tomorrow; tomorrow will look after itself. Each day has troubles enough of its own' (Matthew 6.34).

4 Beauty and freedom

When I was still small, one of my parents' most treasured gifts to me were motor-car rides into the country. In the countryside surrounding a large industrial city my awareness was caught up from my own unhappiness as I was transported to a peak of ineffable joy, a pleasure beyond any verbal description, as my eyes feasted on a beauty beyond human contrivance. My first quite natural reaction was wanting to possess the lovely flowers and shrubs, but even before I could contemplate the action of cutting them, a distinctly higher consciousness forbade me to do anything so destructive, for it revealed, admittedly in embryo understanding, the secret of beauty on a cosmic scale. What is beautiful is a pale image of the Creator's nature, and the more it is preserved and shared with our fellow creatures, the more beautifully does the presence of the Creator shine upon and bless the whole world, and help to transfigure even the meanest creature into something of the nature of its Creator. This means that beauty attains its fullness when it is shared in ardent joy with our fellow creatures, at first with those who can appreciate it directly as we do, but finally with all sentient life. When I, as an unhappy child, came into contact with natural beauty, I dispensed with all my inhibitions as I blossomed into a new person.

It is of interest that the flowers of the spacious garden of my home, much as I cared for them, never evoked that changed state of consciousness which came spontaneously to me when I was playing in an untamed piece of countryside. God seemed to be present in such a place as pure gift, unmanaged by humans and even thriving in spite of their own plans to use nature as a public adornment. The human has indeed been given dominion over the natural world, but I have learned what I had already grasped as a child, that as one grows in mystical awareness, so one leaves the pattern of the natural scene well alone. One strives rather to preserve its beauty than to alter the natural order to suit human aspirations. The way the human exults most gloriously in the natural order is by reproducing it in the form of great art. I would, of course, agree that great landscape gardens do form a point of contact between the beauty of nature and the imagination of the human mind, but can any human contrivance emulate the breathtaking beauty of the purple heather on the Yorkshire moors in early and mid-autumn?

Beauty is one of Plato's three ultimate values that bring us towards the light of God in an intellectual mode; the other two are truth and goodness (or love). The perfection of form, colour and sound seen in nature will, if only we let go of the critical faculty, lead us to a summit of self-transcendence where we are swept into a new appreciation of reality in which Creator and creature are one, not by fusion but by union. But there is a beauty in suffering also if the soul of the afflicted one is transfigured by love. It is glorious to see young athletes intent on the game and young women disporting their beauty in the salons of history, but the most compelling beauty of my experience came to me when one no longer young, and blinded by diabetes, came to me for help. The look of patient anticipation on her face has remained with me when the lithe bodies and blooming faces of the young are like so much clear water that has passed under the shadows in a frolicsome stream during a bright late spring day. Thus beauty liberates us from an anxious concern about our own possessions and deficiencies, and brings us to an appreciation of the universal providence of God. The risen Christ in the apparition described in John 20.24–29 proves his reality to doubting Thomas not by his glowing beauty, but by the marks of his crucifixion. Beauty has a truth about it that Keats commented on in his famous pronouncement from the 'Ode on a Grecian Urn': 'Beauty is truth, truth beauty.' He follows this with the observation, 'That is all ye know on earth, and all ye need to know'. Scientists tell us that there is a beautiful economy about the most useful hypotheses involving nuclear physics, a subject that intrigues the educated layman by the analogies some of these hypotheses seem to share with mystical thinking.

To those with eyes that see and ears that hear – I speak in the biblical mode of Isaiah 6.9–10 and 35.5 – the majesty of beauty is also its consolation to a wounded heart and a depressed mind. Beauty evokes an emotional response by lifting us above our accustomed station in life and seating us with the mighty ones. I am not speaking here about a temporal aristocracy but about the communion of souls who have lived at various times and in diverse circumstances, but have been formed emotionally and spiritually by the beauty that is now ours for a short lifetime – for even if we live to a ripe old age, what is this compared to the everlasting glory of God's grace bestowed on even the smallest of his creatures! In Psalm 29.2 we read the lovely injunction (in the Authorized Version), 'Worship the Lord in the beauty of holiness'. The sentence recurs in Psalm 96.9 and in 1 Chronicles 16.29. The modern versions of the Bible are rather more explicit but so much less beautiful. The Revised English Bible reads, 'In holy attire worship the Lord'. The New Jerusalem Bible reads, 'Adore Yahweh in the splendour of holiness', a pleasant return from a more esoteric translation in the older Standard Version, 'Worship Yahweh in his sacred court', the sacred court being heaven, the invisible counterpart of the Temple of Jerusalem. The beauty, or splendour, of holiness includes not only priestly vestments but also the architecture of the place of worship, the glorious music and the odour of burning incense. All of these lift up the worshipper in the company of the angelic hosts and the great communion of saints, of whom we worshippers are junior members. The worshippers, however nondescript they may appear, are also contributors to the beauty of the scene provided their prayer is rapt and they lose their ego consciousness – often miscalled themselves – in the glory of the scene. Of course God is omnipresent, wherever two or three are gathered together in his name (Matthew 18.20), but a magnificent congregation assembled with a single intent strengthens the divine communion.

The psalms quoted stress the beauty of holiness, but the obverse side of the coin, the holiness of beauty, also demands scrutiny. The concept has been brought to my notice by the distinguished sculptress Josefina de Vasconcellas, whose work has ennobled quite a number of churches. Inasmuch as beauty is wrought by the power of the Holy Spirit through the agency of specially gifted people, whether musicians, artists or writers, the product has a divine essence. This is in fact the supreme value of art: it lifts the consciousness of those who are sensitive to the call of beauty to the presence of God. This applies not only to places of worship as noted in the psalms quoted above, but also, and much more pertinently, to the world of vicious competition, struggle, rejection, and final triumph of the human spirit over all material adversities.

The poignancy of beauty, it has always seemed to me, finds its fulfilment in the human spirit, where the things of the world are transmuted into the symbols of music, visual art and literature. Here the mind reacts to the outer world in terms of its own emotional experience and need. To those blessed with musical ears the whole range of human emotion lies almost unbearably revealed. It strikes an echo in such people's experience, perhaps far beyond what they can articulate rationally, and brings them to the very heart of meaning in a dark life or else one of suffused joy. Above all a spark of hope comes to illuminate a dark shadow of depression, so enabling life to go on rather than halt at a mountain of futility. In my own life, catholic as my musical appreciation has been, it is the inspiration of Mozart, Beethoven and Schubert that has been my greatest support in times of barely penetrable darkness. I love Mozart for the gentle, and sometimes not so gentle, play of light and shade that eloquently illuminates his mature piano concertos. They sometimes seem to come from nowhere, the inspiration, in other words, arriving from a source of divine simplicity and sweeping all earthly dross that we mistakenly call success miles away from reality. The modulations remind me of my own life of struggle and final victory in an achievement that seems to have little to do with me personally. And so I derived hope from them when I was feeling very low in the past, wondering whether I was ever to make the grade and do the task set before me. That task was to fulfil the work ahead of me by making the right contacts who could recognize my potential sufficiently to direct me towards the best channels for my future endeavours. All this sounds disgustingly egoistical, but when one is alone in the world one needs supernatural encouragement to do the nameless work ahead, even if, paradoxically, the task is merely mundane. But the mundane side was to be essentially a foil for something far more significant, to which I could not give a name at that time. And so the glorious genius of Mozart gave me strength and encouragement. The other aspect of Mozart that is especially dear to me are the Viennese operas with their scintillating humour among which a much more serious feeling is silhouetted. It reminds me to take nothing too seriously, at least in an earthly perspective. And so the concertos, symphonies, operas, and the glorious quartets and quintets of this celestial master have been my companions in all emotional weathers, reminding me of one, a genius beyond compare, dead without much notice but inspiring countless millions to a new aspiration of perfection.

The late quartets and sonatas of Schubert have helped me to articulate my periods of gloom in a beauty that defies description, and yet at the end there lay hope of a better future at present wrapped up in terrifying potentialities. The darkness had within it the seed of a new creation which I could somehow grasp, albeit enveloped in gloom through which tiny chinks of light shone in faint encouragement. When these appearances of light occur in one's own psyche, one is inclined to see them as sparks of illusion, but when they are portrayed by a great composer, one knows that one is not alone, and that hope lies in the way; Schubert died miserably but his music consoles the world as two centuries succeeding his life-time slowly approach. And then by complete contrast there sounds his great C major symphony, a work of youthful vision, courage and splendour, wiping away all the tears of doubt and dejection.

This thought brings me to Beethoven, the messenger of heroism *par excellence*. His works were of enormous encouragement in my earlier years, as they still are, but now the 'third period' quartets are my special joy. Here is a completely deaf, ageing man communing with eternity through the lucidity of a soundless mind. He brings me a peace that puts all my emotional struggles and spiritual aspirations in their right perspective before God, who knows us all as we really are, and blesses us with his undemanding love no matter how we have behaved ourselves. It is our joy to receive that love, undisturbed by any personal doubt, like the little children who alone can enter heaven. I suspect that we all have to experience renunciation before that peace can be with us. In order to receive fully, we have to be completely empty of ego consciousness. It could well be that the experience of depression is here to teach us about renunciation. Certainly many depressive people have an enormous creative urge.

I have also known the inspiration of great painting and poetry, but somehow music can say in a few bars what writing and visual art enunciate so much more clumsily in their medium of expression. I shall nevertheless always be grateful for Rembrandt and Goya for bringing me to a finer appreciation of the human spirit, and the French Impressionists for drawing that spirit in its most universal mode. In the use of words, my own medium of communication, how easily one can distinguish between those who know God and the human spirit and those whose work is purely decorative! Once again it is the painting of moods that is the acid test; some writing speaks directly to my condition, whether one of happiness or despondency, whereas other literature simply bores me with its wordiness, as I may well do others in my turn. Apart from the older classics I have found the work of T. S. Eliot, Philip Larkin, and R. S. Thomas to be especially helpful in my own labile emotional moods. Beauty needs no apology, but if it is working to its best it raises the human spirit to the divine essence, in so doing also restoring the human to something of the divine image in which he or she is created, no matter how far from this state they may have wandered during a life of selfishness and cruelty.

It would be reassuring to proclaim that beauty is as inevitably related to goodness as to truth, in the thought of John Keats. Unfortunately this is not so; great villains in history have quite often been admirers of art, sometimes indeed patrons, and also music lovers. Adolf Hitler had an almost god-like admiration for the operas of Richard Wagner. Admittedly they shared strong racial prejudices, but the sublime genius of the composer shines out in the history of Western music even if some of it was misused in the Nazi concentration camps. Few of the world's great artists, whether musical, pictorial or literary, have been especially admirable men, so much so that one gasps with relief when one thinks of J. S. Bach and Joseph Haydn in the sphere of music. Nevertheless the genius of high creativity selects whom it will, no doubt under the aegis of the Holy Spirit, and we should be grateful for the service rendered to the world by even the most flawed artists, scientists and philosophers. They have dedicated their lives to the pursuit of beauty or truth, and their work will remain long after their lives pass into the realm of legend.

The work of goodness, or love, is, however, of a different stamp. If one's life is devoted to the condition of the world as a living organism with humans at the helm, one's first task is inner purification, so that the ego with its demands for recognition and satisfaction may be stilled and steadily civilized. When one's own desire-life has been purged of all personal motives, far easier said than done, then the desire for the transformation of society can be pursued both in safety and with a promise of effectiveness. Love will never rest until beauty, truth and goodness illuminate society. Needless to say, this enormous endeavour starts with oneself, that the beam may be removed from one's own eye in order to see more clearly what has to be done in respect of other people's welfare. A most important part of the work of bringing healing to the world is what may be called a divine darkness, or ignorance: one does not know how to proceed or even the nature of the change that is to be wrought. As soon as one knows with the assertive will, one inevitably tries to influence people and events according to one's own egoistical desires. Once one is inwardly purified, a work of suffering no less than selfless service, one may become an instrument of God and do what is required according to the inspiration of the Holy Spirit. Then does a beauty beyond description flow from one as it illuminates one's features to something of the Christ who is within all of us, our hope of glory (Colossians 1.27). This is something of the nature of a transfiguration that the three disciples witnessed in the ministry of Jesus (Mark 9.2–8). It was also seen in the face of the proto-martyr Stephen as he preached his final sermon (Acts 6.15).

Beauty brings with it freedom from the sordid routine of mundane existence with its emphasis on self-assertiveness. It lifts one's mind beyond the limits of rational thought to the vast expanses of idealized imagination where a new kind of living becomes possible. It does not necessarily bring sanctity with it, since it is still within the grasp of the selfish desire that we all know. But how much more thrilling it is to attend a live concert or opera, even if the performance is not faultless, than to listen to a completely impeccable recording with no audience interaction! All involved add their quota of life to something beyond mere rational perception, the audience no less than the players. As was mentioned at the beginning of the chapter, the more we can share the good things of life with our fellow creatures, the more do they reflect the presence of the Creator on whose love all life depends and all beauty pours forth. I sometimes think of a millionaire with a collection of priceless masterpieces in his strong room. No one can view them except after prior appointment. He is never completely at ease, imagining how a gang of robbers might raid his estate and carry off the art treasures. And so he becomes the prisoner of the masterpieces while they at the same time are his prisoners. How sad and how futile such ownership is! Then let us imagine the owner dying, and his collection passing into the hands of various public collections. Now at last the masterpieces are available to the public, and in their own way they glow with a recognition that was absent when they were sequestered in a rich man's home. It is so with all that is beautiful. It fulfils no useful function inasmuch as it will not play its part in the technological advance of society or aid in humanity's money-making activities. It is there as a witness to an aspect of reality that lies beyond the purely materialistic, and it transports people who are open to its challenge to that greater life, where they may begin to function as real creatures of light, created incredibly in the divine image, as we read in Genesis 1.27.

What this may mean is suggested in the fourth song of the servant of God in Isaiah 52.13 to 53.1–12. It is the great 'suffering servant' passage, which indicates that the hero in his affliction for the saving of humanity is bereft of all beauty. He shows the nature of self-giving love and patient sacrifice, and in that revelation a new type of beauty emerges. This is the soul of the human with the spirit burning ardently within it. The Holy Spirit has brought all that composes a person, body, mind and soul, into unity under the control of the spirit, from where the Holy Spirit illuminates the whole in the form of a new creation, Christ himself. It is in this spiritualized beauty that truth and love can find their realization, as the fulfilled person emerges from the flames of torture to the life of eternity.

He has out-soared the shadow of our night;
Envy and calumny and hate and pain,
And that unrest which men miscall delight,
Can touch him not and torture not again;
From the contagion of the world's slow stain
He is secure, and now can never mourn
A heart grown cold, a head grown grey in vain.

These lines come from Shelley's 'Adonais', an elegy to his friend John Keats.

5 The pain of the world

It is both a great privilege and an almost unbearable sorrow to live in our world. Its natural beauty cannot but arrest the thoughts of anyone who is not completely steeped in their own concerns. But that beauty is caught in the flow of nature, from its fragile birth in spring, its flowering in summer, its crowning colour in autumn, and then the dropping of leaves, the death of flowers, and the final stark bareness of winter. The daylight recedes to a night that embraces the early hours of the working day and the retiring afternoon. We accept all this without great thought, knowing full well that a new spring will in due course open a fresh year of fecundity, heralded by the snowdrops and crocuses to be followed by the daffodils and tulips that in turn usher in the full efflorescence of early summer, the most beautiful time of freshness and glorious vegetation. How sad it is when we contemplate the tracts of fertile nature that have been ravished by covetous humans, and converted into vast deserts of dreary factories and featureless dwellings! But, it may be objected, these are the life-blood of society, without which not only would humans starve to death, but nature itself run to ruin. I have tried to dispel this second objection in the last chapter, but the first is less easily dismissed. Civilization entails the building of cities, and these in turn encroach on the land around them. At present technology is so far advanced that it threatens to take over the whole world; humans are admittedly in charge but they are less often in complete control, inasmuch as the power contained in vast industrial works fills the owners with so great a feeling of grandeur that they can scarcely prevent themselves being led along the path of even greater development almost as a challenge to their rivals and to nature itself.

Is industrial development therefore intrinsically wrong? I think this question requires a deeper consideration. The human species is meant to develop its potential, a gift that resides in a superbly developed brain (and one also liable to depressive disease in unfortunate people) which will never be satisfied until the pillars of creation have been laid bare, scaled, and formed the foundation for further advances into the unknown. The moralist will term this attitude hubris, an insolent, overweening pride leading to nemesis. This is retributive justice ending in a well-deserved downfall. The biblical analogue is the story of the Tower of Babel recounted in Genesis 11.1–9. If the search for truth can be effected in a spirit of awe for a creation beyond human calculation, then the work may be pursued beneficially for nature as well as the human mind, but if there is no respect for the unknown, tragedy is sure to follow. The ultimate theme of the Wisdom Literature of the Bible is 'The fear of the Lord is the beginning of wisdom' (Proverbs 1.7; Psalm 111.10; Job 28.28; Ecclesiasticus 1.14). This fear is not the anxiety before an unpredictable tyrant, but the awe one feels when one is with something too great to be defined which one knows intuitively to be holy. There is admittedly no clinching intellectual proof of God, for God is known primarily in the heart (affect) and only secondarily with the mind (reason). The workings of the universe are increasingly open to scientific scrutiny and analysis, but how and why it existed in the first place remains a mystery. Creation, in other words, is not intellectually explicable even though its workings are within the range of the human mind. This beneficent mystery fills the sensitive person with awe. When we can register this awe we fulfil the humanity within us, and expand spiritually into something of the nature of the divine.

Holiness is a quality of people close to the God of all creation, and it shows itself in a Christ-like character. It is the prerogative of the saints of all the religious traditions. By contrast, virtue incorporates a way of life that faithfully observes the moral law. In itself it is beyond praise, but unless it embraces the supreme quality of love, it may become hard and judgemental. A number of Jesus' parables and encounters in daily life demonstrate the inadequacy of a virtuous life that has no love at its centre (Luke 7.36–50, 15.11–32, 18.9–14). The type of person who has felt awe on special occasions is bound to be open to the impress of love even if their moral life is not impeccable. Awe informs one of one's smallness before the mystery of creation; it inculcates humility which is the portal through which love can enter the personality and from which it may proceed to serve one's neighbour. This service is a combination of God's inspiration and one's own capability. No wonder the awe of God is the beginning of a wisdom that can serve the world quietly and without fuss or egoistical display. If one knows this awe, the burden of self-conscious posturing falls away, and one can enjoy the vibrant creation with the abandon of a small child.

Meister Eckhart goes so far as to say that in our world God requires us humans just as much as we require him. This does not mean that we are God's equals in power or wisdom, but simply that the divine will has decreed that we are created in the divine image and that we are to work in harmony, even partnership, with the Creator. If we are attuned to the will of God in a life of prayer, we shall do what is right not only for ourselves but for the whole world (and, I believe, the greater universe as well because of the far-ranging power of prayer). The spirit of awe makes us commune spontaneously with God by the action of prayer, which is to be seen primarily as listening to the divine source in quiet contemplation. From all this it becomes evident that the perfect state of mind is one of peace, a freedom from personal striving so that all our efforts can be devoted to the service of those around us. The end of all this is a beatitude in which we may together do the work of governing the world to the benefit of the entire creation. Moods of happiness are by the nature of mundane existence bound to be evanescent, as darkness follows light and death ends even the most glorious life. It may well be that a positive pleasure is preferable to a negative sadness, but both are necessary for the growth of the personality from childish self-centredness to an adult responsibility that can take under its wing the less fortunate members of the created order, who will certainly include ourselves as we approach the waning years of diminishment, to use a favourite Teilhardian concept.

It is evident that our mood, or state of mind, has both an endogenous (internal) and an exogenous (external) component. The condition of our body will affect the cheerfulness of our mood; thus chronic ill-health, especially if there is severe pain that does not respond adequately to treatment, soon leads to a state of dejection, which may progress to desperation if there is no relief. Desperation is a state of such abandonment of hope that any chance may be taken no matter how reckless it may appear. It has a positive aspect no matter how grave the situation may be. The related mood of despair is entirely negative: the abandonment of hope is absolute and the person sinks into apathy and sometimes a suicidal frame of mind. It is a concomitant of severe depression, but can also occur in the normally functioning individual when the dice of fate seems inexorably loaded against him or her. One thinks of the victims of concentration camps facing certain extermination, or a patient with a lethal disease at death's door. In these cases it not infrequently happens that a braver face is shown as death is about to close the scene. Personally I believe that entities from the other side of life are at this juncture approaching to lead the dying individual to a happier existence of which we can barely speak from the virtual blindness of mortal life.

One thing is certain: no matter how extravert (or outward-looking) our personality may be, we are soon turned sharply upon ourselves when we are in physical pain or when the world and its fortunes go wrong for us. The natural introvert, one whose attention is constantly drawn inwardly to his or her condition, is less overwhelmed by adverse circumstances, because in a way they are unconsciously prepared for them. I am a very typical introvert, and this has helped me to resonate with the problems of other people more easily than I would had I been so outward-looking that I could hardly have articulated in depth with anyone. But, on the other hand, I have had difficulty with superficial social relationships as a result of both my shyness and an awareness of deeper matters than those that usually impinge on most other people, until, of course, disaster strikes. No one personality type is preferable to another; what matters is how we make use of our gifts and strive to strengthen, or at least compensate for, weak functions in our constitution.

In Jungian thought there are, in addition to introversion and extraversion, four psychological types of personality depending on the four 'functions': sensation, direct perception of what is going on by the senses; thinking, the ability to fit pieces of information logically by reason; feeling, assessing matters according to value judgements; and intuition, the ability to see beyond the tangibles in a situation to hidden factors. Indeed, intuition comes to us by information that is transmitted by the unconscious. Sensation and intuition are separate ways of perceiving a situation, whereas thinking and feeling are separate ways of assessing it. In a fully rounded person these functions are properly balanced. The experience of fully conscious awareness makes us more open to information acquired intuitively; reverses of one type or another seem to be mandatory for us to be aware of ourselves in relation to the world around us – neither to be lost in our own speculations nor to be immersed in the attraction of outside events to the extent of being passively carried along with them.

Great spiritual teachers have repeatedly drawn their disciples' attention to living in the present moment, which is both the here and now and also the point of eternity in the experience of time. Jean-Pierre de Caussade, an eighteenth-century Jesuit spiritual director, in his classic *Self-Abandonment to Divine Providence* speaks cogently about 'the sacrament of the present moment'. But it is a sacrament only if we are fully there to receive it; Christ is in fact the eternal celebrant, and he offers us his presence and the divine wisdom that proceeds from it without condition and with full love. 'He was in the world; but the world, though it owed its being to him, did not recognize him. He came to his own, and his people would not accept him. But to all who did accept him, to those who put their trust in him, he gave the right to become children of God, born not of human stock, by the physical desire of a human father, but of God' (John 1.10–13). To me this momentous statement about the event and effect of the Incarnation is much more than simply the delineation of a new, and major, religious denomination. It speaks to me of the renewed humanity of all those who have the humility, self-control, and dedication to their fellows to give fully of themselves moment by moment of their mortal lives. Such a person has truly followed the example of Christ and has as a consequence been filled fully with his grace. That grace is the power that integrates the personality to allow the great individuation process, described by Jung, slowly to take form. Here we have a creative synthesis between the polarities of the personality with a living integration of the conscious mind and its great unconscious background. When humanity has attained this spiritual understanding there will indeed be peace on earth and goodwill towards all creatures. Experiencing the world's pain both as onlookers and as sufferers causes us to attain a greater understanding of life as it is, and a more effective means of participating in that life. But then we are transformed individuals; the beam has been effectively removed from our own eyes, and we can see the problems confronting the world more precisely, so that our efforts may in truth help in the redemption of life from sickness to health. In other words, as we move beyond the sin of personal separation to the virtue of corporate action, we grasp the liberating function of service for the world and become transformed people.

The concepts of service and duty need to be thoroughly analysed. There is a type of service that is grudgingly drawn out of one. We recall the Parable of the Importunate Friend in Luke 11.5–8: a householder is awoken in the middle of the night by a friend who asks for food for another friend who has suddenly turned up and requires urgent hospitality. The householder is very grumpy at being so disturbed from his sleep, but finally yields to his friend's entreaty and provides food for him. He does this service with a poor grace, whereas his friend performed his service in a spirit of caring and solicitude. If one serves for any reason other than love, the work is not psychically fulfilled even if the material result is satisfactory. In other words, service is intimately involved in personal relationships: in the story recounted above, the householder has not related properly to his friend, who in turn has taken the food in an unhappy spirit.

Nevertheless, the thought of his other friend receiving the food with gratitude serves to bring him up to a joyful satisfaction as he speedily returns to his home. It is better to serve with a bad grace than to withdraw from the work, for, apart from helping in an immediate capacity, the habit of serving another person will gradually impress itself on one's way of life, and the happiness that one gives to another will reflect itself on to one's own character. This is in fact the way of effecting good relationships with a multitude of different people. 'All real living is meeting': we remember Martin Buber's aphorism from Chapter 2.

We live by duty and discipline, but if these are treated as an end in themselves, they become heartless tyrants. Duty and discipline properly understood and undertaken play an essential part in the maturation of the personality, and in exceptional people its perfection also. To bring peace, however temporary, to a troubled soul is the greatest joy that an aspiring person can know. As Jesus puts it in the Parable of the Prodigal Son, 'How could we fail to celebrate this happy day? Your brother here was dead and has come back to life; he was lost and has been found' (Luke 15.32). Service properly performed brings joy to giver and recipient alike because it breaks down barriers of class and social distinction on the one hand and stubborn pride on the other. Then both parties start to function as real humans, losing their small concerns in a relationship that brings both to the foothills of the divine nature. Service is the obverse side of growth on the coin of personal sanctification. It may be that 'happiness lies more in giving than in receiving' (Acts 20.35), but it is also important to be able to receive with graciousness and gratitude. Giving implies strength, which is always satisfying to show; receiving indicates weakness, which a self-sufficient person is loath to admit even to himself or herself, let alone a benefactor.

When a duty becomes part of one's style of living, and discipline brings with it a constant life of prayer, one can see fully the necessity for both these qualities in the development of the personality to Christ-like proportions. It needs also to be said that our first duty is towards our own well-being, because only when we are in health of body and mind can we perform our duty to our neighbour. Discipline keeps us on the right path especially when we are tempted by the world's various distractions. Discipline strengthens the will, so that we may be masters of various situations, even those that are extremely painful, rather than being wafted like autumn leaves falling to the ground and blown hither and thither by the indifferent wind. There comes a time in our lives when ageing and poor health limit our activities to the extent that we depend increasingly on the service of others, both our friends and professional carers. Our duty now is to practise patience and forbearance, trying to make the work of these people as pleasant as possible by being cheerful even when events in and around us are disheartening. The practice of contemplative prayer can be a veritable lifeline in these circum-stances. I have previously noted how my intercession work helped me so well when I had the severe attack of depression that I described in the first chapter. In other words, the more we can turn our attention from our own troubles to those of other people, the more constructively can we live in times of difficulty, and the more we can cultivate the sincere concern of others for our own condition. Our old age shows the fruit of our spiritual life-style (or lack of it) in the love that other people bestow upon us. So let us give thanks to God for the Law that teaches us our various duties to ourselves and our fellows, remembering that love is the fulfilment of the law (Romans 13.10). As we fulfil the law so we become integrated into society, of which we are a constituent, unique member. Our unique contribution is our way of personal growth and also a means of enriching the whole. The law, assuming it is just, gives us an invaluable guideline, but it is not self-fulfilling. It is the Spirit of God within us that moves us on the way, and the example of other people encourages us on our path. It is a great consolation to be carried by the weight of opinion along certain moral paths, but nothing dare be taken for granted, as the life and ministry of Jesus showed the world. The great lesson of any life is the priority of love above all else, and it is the occasional conflict between law and love that contributes to life's poignancy; the lover has to learn to love his or her adversaries, and this is both extremely difficult and the heart of the creative path.

Some temperaments are open to circumstances and are naturally happy. Others walk in the shadows and are naturally melancholy. The artist has a melancholy core, being aware of the tragic impermanence of beauty in the face of the relentless passage of the seasons of life that are mirrored in the changes inevitable in each passing year. But whereas nature has the capacity to renew itself each spring, the path of human life is ceaselessly onwards towards maturity, senescence and death. We can either accept this with a shrug of the shoulders and then pass onwards oblivious of everything except our own selfish concerns, or else we may become deeply involved in the natural scene and experience a melancholy turn of mind that may, if the situation does not right itself, progress to dejection and despondency. Such moods of melancholy, dejection, and despondency all lie within the normal range when one grieves over human cruelty and natural disasters. They are not to be equated with clinical depression with its characteristic lack of self-worth and its crippling of the whole mode of self-expression except in negative categories. The term melancholia can be equated with depression, but it is not used in modern psychiatric terminology; it belongs to a past age of medical practice.

The temperament may be thought of as the result of our whole bodily constitution on our way of confronting the world – in action, emotion and thought. The ancients classified temperament in terms of the four 'humours', which were blood, phlegm, yellow bile and black bile. The first alludes to the sanguine type of person, whose disposition is hopeful and courageous; the second to a sluggish rather apathetic individual, who is described as phlegmatic. The choleric (yellow bile) temperament is angry and irascible, whereas the melancholic (black bile) temperament moves towards pensive sadness. We no longer think of temperament in terms of the body's fluids, but the four types of temperament thus delineated are still worthy of reflection if only in a poetic context. It would be wrong to identify the melancholic group *par excellence* with depression, for the other three are also liable to this affliction. A number of fine humorists have tragically ended their lives in a fit of suicidal depression.

There are certain times in the year when one feels very unhappy. A notable one is the period leading up to Christmas, the family holiday with a vengeance. For those of us who live alone and are alone in an indifferent society, the emptiness can be almost intolerable. I myself have no family in Britain, and so I feel for the numerous people who have no home at all worth living in. To be sure I am given much hospitality commensurate with my work as a priest and writer, but the time of leaving to return to an empty flat has its own sadness which cannot be erased. What a privilege it is to share that aloneness with many millions of other people whose living conditions are quite appalling, unlike my own very comfortable flat! T. S. Eliot writes at the beginning of *The Waste Land*:

April is the cruellest month, breeding
Lilacs out of the dead land, mixing
Memory and desire, stirring
Dull roots with spring rain.

He compares this with a paradoxically warm winter under snow-bound earth and a rainy, sunlit summer full of life. Indeed, in spring the world around us starts to move from the previous decay to the beginning of a new life. But the depressive type of individual becomes stuck in the old ways, while the world passes on to blossoms and flowers. No wonder spring is so cruel for those who are prevented from living. But there is always the joy of appreciating a new birth, at least for those whose minds are supple even if their bodies are failing under the burden of disease and the accretion of years. The pain of the world, as we feel it, is acutely related to our own mood, which in turn is a resultant of our temperament, our state of health, and the attitudes of those around us, especially those with whom we are in close relationship.

Some people are naturally optimistic, believing that in the end good will prevail over evil. They tend to have a sanguine temperament, and have a cheerful view of life. Others are naturally pessimistic, tending to see the worst in all situations and having a gloomy view about the future of humanity and the world. These are by no means all of melancholy disposition. Angry and phlegmatic types of people often express pessimistic views, and there are some groups who gain enormous pleasure from giving or attending pessimistic dissertations on the future of society or the world order. I myself have a somewhat paradoxical temperament that embraces both melancholy and sanguine elements, and though I am subject to periods of depression and am intimately involved with people who are in serious mental and physical ill-health, any feeling of pessimism is soon overridden by a glorious optimism that all is well in God's care despite material evidence to the contrary. It is my faith in God and my admiration for suffering humanity that give me a hopeful view of life. As St Paul puts it in Romans 8.28, 'And, as we know, all things work together for good for those who love God'. The essence of this declaration is the love of God. This shows itself in the lives of many agnostic types of people by the caring they bestow on their fellow creatures – which to some extent includes all that lives. Our love of God is measured by the depth of our love for our fellow creatures. If our love of God leads us to hurt all those who do not subscribe to our own faith, we may be sure that the object of our devotion is not the Deity but some subordinate psychic entity which has successfully mimicked God, not a very difficult thing to do since no one has ever seen God fully at any time.

The sentiments expressed in Tennyson's poem 'Break, Break, Break' speak of the nobility of the human spirit as it confronts the facts of life and eternity day by day.

Break, break, break,
On thy cold gray stones, O Sea!
And I would that my tongue could utter
The thoughts that arise in me.

O well for the fisherman's boy,
That he shouts with his sister at play!
O well for the sailor lad,
That he sings in his boat on the bay!

And the stately ships go on
To their haven under the hill;
But O for the touch of a vanished hand,
And the sound of a voice that is still!

Break, break, break,
At the foot of thy crags, O Sea!
But the tender grace of a day that is dead
Will never come back to me.

The transient quality of mortal life infuses it with an ineffable beauty, though the greatest music effortlessly captures the mood. The composer must have known the agony of unbridged separation before the notes could sound true. We frail humans look for the ultimate union of that separation, despite the arrogant disdain of the unimaginative mind. This union starts now as the creative impulse renews our character, progressing to the life beyond death which comes to us in unheralded glimpses which at present can scarcely be articulated let alone confided to our fellows. The end of the process is such an openness to God that his love transfigures our bodies. From them flows a blessing that brings peace to all whom we meet in our daily work. All the moods that the pain of the world evokes work together for our re-creation as servants of God, so that we may strive for the transformation of the world from a place of sordid commerce to a vale of transcendent beauty.

So let us finally immerse ourselves in the fount of Blake's 'The Divine Image':

To Mercy, Pity, Peace, and Love
All pray in their distress;
And to these virtues of delight
Return their thankfulness.

For Mercy, Pity, Peace, and Love,
Is God, our father dear,
And Mercy, Pity, Peace, and Love,
Is Man, His child and care.

For Mercy has a human heart,
Pity a human face,
And Love, the human form divine,
And Peace, the human dress.

Then every man, of every clime,
That prays in his distress,

Prays to the human form divine,
Love, Mercy, Pity, Peace.

And all must love the human form,
In heathen, turk or jew;
Where Mercy, Love, & Pity dwell
There God is dwelling too.

6 The hope that does not pale

Traversing the darkness of so much of our mortal life we are kept on course by the inner conviction that a happy conclusion will be reached. Dame Julian of Norwich was taught in her *Revelations of Divine Love* that sin is necessary, but that all will be well in the fullness of time. The solution of this paradox, that sin is an integral part of life, lies in its being the portal of entry of forgiveness, whereby we alone may experience love and know its real meaning. Some of Jesus' encounters and parables illuminate this situation: the prodigal son, for instance, is received home rapturously by his rejoicing father, although he knows full well that he deserves humiliating reproof such as his older brother would gladly provide. But returning home to unrestrained rejoicing effects a juxtaposition of forgiveness and love into a previously selfish life, one that had regarded the satisfaction of carnal lusts as the *summum bonum* of a fruitful existence. When the Holy Spirit spoke in the depths of his soul while he was languishing in destitution, he came to himself in freedom from a hell of hedonism that had sown the seed of its own imprisonment. Then he was able to return home to whatever reception he might encounter (Luke 15.11–32).

This is how hope manifests itself when it suddenly bursts upon one during a period of despondency: there is an expansion felt in the region of the heart, the part of the body where affect manifests itself. In this way the vile experience of inner closure is relieved, as if a locked door is opened by a key and the soul exposed to the light of day. It is in this mood that one can concur with Dame Julian's conviction that all will be well; indeed all is well in eternity even if the present situation is painful. This openness to hope is dulled during a period of depression. No matter how sincere the encouragement of the sympathetic onlooker, how insistent may be the message of good tidings, the depressed person remains emotionally unmoved. It seems as if the information cannot penetrate the shut psychic portals through which emotional information reaches the mind. It is noteworthy that St John of the Cross described a not dissimilar state of affairs in what he called 'the dark night of the spirit' (a state later than the better-known 'dark night of the soul'), in which all spiritual consolation is powerless to penetrate the obfuscation enfolding the soul. The pain was not mitigated by well-meaning spiritual directors assuring him that all was in order, when he himself knew the matter to be the reverse, and the directors ignorant of his condition. The question arises as to whether the saint was describing a period of clinical depression or whether the experience was part of the spiritual journey of the soul to God, in a terrain where all spiritual light was necessarily occluded. Only thus would one know God in the divine darkness not only of the reasoning mind but also of the soul.

I believe the latter, that St John's experience was a grim part of his journey to God, who is beyond all description and is known to the mystic in negative categories, for no one can see God directly and remain alive. We begin to know God by his emergent energies of which love and light are the two compelling ones. But the mystic knows even more than these, for God is above all else the absolute nothing, 'the cloud of unknowing' in terms of the title of a famous mystical treatise by an anonymous medieval English writer. The demeanour of the saint appears to be something more than that of a clinically depressed person. But it could well be that he had a depressive tendency. Whereas most depressives would remain helpless in their agony, he was able to use it in his spiritual journey. This illustrates something that we encounter repeatedly in our investigation of depression, that the condition is multifactorial, there being a number of factors involved in its causation.

To me the most terrible experience of depression encountered in the history of the Spirit is Jesus' grappling with demonic forces while he was in Gethsemane. He had some insight into the nature of his coming trial after the Passover meal during which he instituted the Eucharist, and so he chose his three most intimate disciples (Peter, John and James) to accompany him for what was about to occur. They were completely out of their depth, and were simply not with their Master during the time at Gethsemane. Jesus was effectively alone, and the struggle was of terrifying scale. But he prevailed in his conflict with cosmic evil, and was ready for the mosaic of events that followed. Here then is yet another factor in the development of depression: psychic conflict with demonic forces.

Hope is the most intimate of inner feelings; it comprises a combination of desire and expectation. This factor of anticipation separates hope from mere wishful thinking. In other words the end of hope is faith, which in terms of its famous definition in Hebrews 11.1 (in the Authorized Version) is the substance of things hoped for, the evidence of things not seen. In a more recent version faith is described as giving substance to our hopes and convincing us of realities we do not see. From all this it is evident that hope is the primary emotion. It gives birth to faith which shows itself in action: making our hopes realities by the exercise of the will. Faith is an active way to accomplishment, whereas belief is essentially an intellectual expression of certain articles of faith. One can, for instance, repeat the Creed daily, but until it becomes a clarion call to action, it remains purely theoretical.

Hope is like the first rays of the sun breaking through the darkness of a lengthy night and lighting up the previously hidden landscape to reveal its naked beauty. It comes to us all after some well-deserved humiliation, when we can hardly bear to show ourselves to our fellows. The emotion evoked is that of shame, and we wonder whether we will ever be able to face the world again. Those of low spiritual awareness will thrust themselves against the outer world with heedless insistence, showing what we call a brave face, and sometimes a shameless one too. But their behaviour is noticed, albeit frequently unconsciously, by others, for nothing that is done fails to evoke its corresponding reaction. On the other hand, the sensitive type of person will tend to hide himself or herself in the shadows in order to arouse as little comment as possible. And then the emergent rays of hope suddenly penetrate the darkness and illuminate it with the forgiveness that is divine in origin. The humiliated individual can now show themself to the world, and admit their fault without excuse. It is quite clear to me that they are accompanied by their guardian angel, God's messenger allotted to their particular care, and now their self-esteem is supported from a source much more exalted than any human agency. I believe categorically in the ministry of angels, who are messengers of God through the agency of the Holy Spirit. Every living organism is supported by its angelic protector, but only the human is capable of appreciating this aid. And even he or she seems often unaware of this support until the ego has been displaced from its customary place of dominance by peril of one kind or another. Humiliation is a great disaster inasmuch it cuts away much of the illusion that clothes the ego, revealing its naked weakness. It is at that moment that truth can penetrate the shaken ego and illuminate the personality that is so often hidden by specious pretension. When we are inwardly illuminated by truth, we suddenly come to see how beautiful we are in the sight of God; this even if our lives have been far from exemplary.

The essence of a happy life is an attitude of self-esteem which allows us to do our work without self-doubt or diffidence. That self should, however, be accepted rather than needing to be constantly affirmed by display or the praise of others. The less I think about myself in the course of my work, the better is the work performed and the greater is my feeling of satisfaction, which shows itself in ever more creative work on behalf of the community. Such work is bound to be less lucrative than private endeavour, but what may be sacrificed in terms of financial reward is returned in general goodwill. At that point I am identified with the whole, and need not assert myself as a private force requiring constant reassurance that all is well with me. 'He who keeps watching the wind will never sow, and he who keeps his eye on the clouds will never reap' (Ecclesiastes 11.4). The essence of a fruitful life is one in which we are so closely united to the world in our endeavour that we can put our trust in the workings of divine grace, by which we are sustained day by day. There are sure to be occasions when disaster strikes, but if we are in one piece with the created order, we will survive and carry on as best as we are able. The story of the trials of Job points the way here, and when death ultimately closes the present scene, we will be ready for further adventures in the life beyond death. All this is an illustration of existence grounded in hope and lived with childlike faith. What is required of one is to serve quietly and with humour for the benefit of the community as a whole; one is supported by unseen forces which act best when one is animated with goodwill and trust, and can give of oneself unaffectedly to the task at hand. All this is a working description of a constructive life, something more than mere happiness, which is at best a fleeting state of affairs and wisely not to be grasped when it comes upon one. There should rather be gratitude to God for what has been given, and the will to continue in humility until the whole has been attained: this is the good life beyond all emotions that points to something of the peace which passes all understanding.

When one can face one's guilt in an attitude of straightforward truth, rather like the prodigal son, and ask God for forgiveness, one is instantly relieved of one's burden and given the strength to move on in contrition to the purpose ahead of one in one's life. 'Come to me, all who are weary and whose load is heavy; I will give you rest' (Matthew 11.28). Christ does this by taking the load upon himself, so that we may have some respite from our inner turmoil, and as he lifts our pain from us, there flows in a golden ray of hope that soon broadens into a band of resolve. Through faith this resolve is actualized, and its substance fulfilled in our future work. The quotation continues, 'Take my yoke upon you, and learn from me, for I am gentle and humble-hearted; and you will find rest for your souls. For my yoke is easy to wear, my load is light' (verses 29–30). In fact the yoke of Christ is the suffering of the whole world and the load the collective sin of humanity since its inception. But transcending all this pain there is an awareness of God, who will lift up the darkness, as Jesus' tortured body was raised at the time of his resurrection, and rain down upon all who are open to life and aware of their fellow creatures a blessing of light and an inner glow of hope that heralds a new way of service and love. Guilt is our emotional response to sin which we freely acknowledge, and shame is the attitude we register to those around us. When we can repeat St Paul's admission, 'For all alike have sinned, and are deprived of the divine glory' (Romans 3.23), the joy of collective forgiveness comes upon us as hope expands our previously closed emotional response and allows the warmth of God's presence to direct our way. St Paul puts this more theologically as he continues, 'and all are justified by God's free grace alone, through his act of liberation in the person of Christ Jesus' (verse 24). This justification, the act of being put in right relationship with God, follows Christ's love for us, and we in turn are freed and directed to show a similar love to our fellows, so that love may abound and hope flourish for what we are destined to achieve for the regeneration of the world.

During the period of the severe depression I had ten years ago I was engaged in writing a book about Christ's presence in the world today, which I entitled *Coming in Glory*. Sadly it is now out of print, but there is a portion of the prologue which is worth quoting.

I felt completely cut off from the usual source of my creativity. Prayer, which is the usual staple of my life, could then be carried out only by rote, for I was encompassed in a darkness that resembled a pea-soup type of fog. At the same time I was excessively sensitive emotionally, and past memories came flooding into my mind; I was overwhelmed by mental pain almost too acute to bear. But I continued praying for others, though no one needed prayer more than I. Suddenly one morning I was aware of a blue light in my spiritual horizon, such as is customary when I normally pray and am involved in the ministry of healing. This was my first indication that I had turned the corner of my depression, and was now able to see something of the spiritual realm once more.

The blue light which lightens the darkness in my prayer life is a pale spark of hope not only for myself but for all those whom I remember in my intercession. I would interpret it as a psychic phenomenon of high spiritual potency, signifying the illumination of the coarse emotional nature by a fine flame of God's cleansing love. This is precisely how hope inspires the psyche in its ever-proceeding course of action, a delicate light of purity that brings the person back again to their childhood innocence. This is the state of mind in which to pursue all creative activity, observing that the heart of creativity lies in relating with integrity to oneself and one's fellow creatures. The arts of music, visual representation, and literature are great products of creative imagination, but even more fundamental is the capacity to relate in open trust to another person. The arts themselves find their full realization in confiding the human spirit intimately to the world, so that people may become ennobled in their work together; the end is a transformed society in which love is the cardinal activity. This is admittedly a visionary aspiration when one considers the darkness of so much of the individual psyche that reached a nadir in the mass destruction of our present century. But hope springs in the most unlikely situations and from the most unprepossessing people whose 'better selves' suddenly perform actions of the greatest heroism and self-sacrificing love. One can say with the Psalmist, 'When I look up at your heavens, the work of your fingers, at the moon and the stars you have set in place, what is a frail mortal, that you should be mindful of him, a human being, that you should take notice of him? Yet you have made him little less than a god, crowning his head with glory and honour' (Psalm 8.3–5). There is hope in even the most desperate situations, and the capacity of a Spirit-filled human is enormous. The greatest work is neither technological marvels nor charismatic phenomena; it is the act of renunciation of the self for the sake of the world, which is concentrated into one's neighbour who is in need. 'Anything you did for one of my brothers here, however insignificant, you did for me' (Matthew 25.40).

Hope stimulates faith which should put one's dearest aspirations into practice. Sometimes, however, faith becomes an end in itself, so that a literalistic view of a Scripture passage ends all discussion about a subject. This type of faith, very common amongst fundamentalists of various religious traditions, smothers hope in that it puts paid to any development of thought that might illuminate the present view with a broader perspective that is not afraid of the insights of modern scientific understanding and the spiritual genius of others of the world's great saints. Certainty puts an end to hope, but where the assurance is only true in part or even frankly erroneous, it quenches the human spirit and precipitates terrible reactions of intolerance, fanaticism and superstition: anyone who cannot subscribe fully to something that at its very best is of tentative nature is regarded as a dangerous heretic whose wrong attitudes may precipitate the wrath of God. The progressive nature of the unfolding of truth is hard for insecure individuals to accept, for they look for absolute certainty. They exclude the marvellous quality of hope from their lives and remain static until their death. Where growth ceases, atrophy and dissolution inevitably follow.

It must also be said that some exponents of modernistic, liberal religion are uncompromisingly reductionist, dogmatically attributing all phenomena to material causes, and contemptuously rejecting the psychic and spiritual nature of at least some human experience. This point of view is equally intolerant, and hope is sadly marginalized and eventually removed from its range of possibility. Anyone who is absolutely sure of a religious position may acquire a warm centre of repose, but if that person is not fully aware, they may find it a coffin also. No wonder we have to become as children if we are to enter the kingdom of Heaven (Matthew 18.3): they retire to bed peacefully each night, and awake in hope to new adventures each morning.

When people are incurably ill, especially those facing imminent death, it is very important for those around them to flow out in reasoned hope. This is not a blind optimism, that all will be well on this side of the grave, but a lightness of touch that seems to put the present sadness in the context of the vast universe. If matters of life and death are broached by the patient, it is wiser to listen than to hold the floor with dogmatic opinions. It seems that many slowly dying patients are given deep information not only about their condition and its probable outcome, but also about those who have recently died and the preparations under way for their own transition to the life beyond physical death.

The same approach is also true for those suffering from clinical depression. These often include a number of bereaved patients. I spoke in Chapter 1 about 'communicative silence', and the heart of the matter lies in understanding the process. I might say that the term was used appreciatively of my company by a person I knew only moderately well, whom I had invited to dinner – her deceased mother with whom I had worked intensively in the ministry of deliverance, and whom I mention again in Chapter 13, was the point of contact, but a similar sort of compliment had been paid before when I was in the company of a woman whom I had previously counselled during a period of difficult family relationship. In this case she had invited me to a dress rehearsal at Glyndebourne, where she worked on the administrative staff. We had a light supper between acts of *Porgy and Bess*, George Gershwin's delightful folk opera.

In each case, and no doubt in many others too, I carried on such a conversation that we both enjoyed, and when the topic came to an end, I was quite happy to remain silent, enjoying the company of my partner and the atmosphere of the surroundings. In due course the conversation was resumed, when an interesting observation struck one of us, but no attempt was made to continue talking at all costs. The silence at first apparently disconcerted my friends, who were accustomed to a continuous flow of talk, but soon they began to relax and, like me, enjoy the moment at hand. It was a new experience for them, and a health-giving one also. I, living alone, am used to silence so much that the noise and conviviality of a party comes as an initial shock to me; likewise when the end of a silent retreat that I have conducted is happily celebrated over the last meal before we all return home. When one is with a clinically depressed person, this communicative silence is like balm to the victim. Somehow one's deep understanding and concern are much more effectively communicated psychically from a spiritual source within one (the 'apex of the soul' where the spirit is situated, and it in turn is the focus of the Holy Spirit in each person), when one is completely silent until the Holy Spirit impels one to say a special word of encouragement or enlightenment. The apogee of com-municative silence is prayer; only when we are quiet before the mystery of creation may the divine presence meet us, because then we are ready to receive God. As we grow in the way of prayer, so do we begin to know that true prayer is an aware openness to the workings of God, that we may play our part in transmitting the divine love to all whom we meet in the daily round. Prayer is universal in scope, for God has no favourites. The way of communicative silence is also the most effective way of knowing God and serving our fellow creatures. Communicative silence transmits hope directly to our depressed friends and indeed to all that bear the burden of misfortune and loneliness. I have little doubt that we will appreciate this silence when the body is dead and the soul passes forth into new surroundings for fresh adventures.

Hope springs eternal in the human breast;
Man never is, but always to be blest.
The soul, uneasy, and confined from home,
Rests and expatiates in a life to come.
Lo, the poor Indian! whose untutored mind
Sees God in clouds, or hears him in the wind;
His soul proud science never taught to stray
Far as the solar walk or milky way;
Yet simple nature to his hope has giv'n,
Behind the cloud-topped hill, an humbler heav'n.

Alexander Pope, *An Essay on Man*, Epistle i, 1, 95

7 Moods of warmth

Beautiful though the world may be, we find our greatest happiness when we are in the company of our own kind, when we can reveal ourselves without inhibition, and relax in the warmth of friendship and the service of love. How many friends have we? The person who is young in the world's ways will identify most of the people he or she knows as a friend, unless, of course, there is manifest hostility between the two of them. This would be the response of a young child; later in childhood and adolescence a friend would be one who shares a common interest in sport or academic studies, especially if the common interest is accompanied by a scarcely definable rapport that makes the one feel at home with the other. The test of a growing friendship is a developing trust that will allow the one to reveal themself more explicitly to the other, and be able in turn to accept and guard the revelations so received.

Friendship is a priceless gift; the true friend is more to be sought than all the prosperity that the world holds dear: prosperity is an evanescent state, whereas the friend will support one up to the portals of death. Jesus says, 'There is no greater love than this, that someone should lay down his life for his friends' (John 15.13). When one views this criterion in terms of the fleeing disciples at the time of the betrayal, one can say with heartfelt sadness that the greatest friend of humanity went to his death bereft of all friends: they took easily enough but they gave little in return. And yet in the very recording of this fact, we see its sheer inadequacy: friendship looks for no response, its free gift is its reward. What a long way we have gone from simple, undiscriminating childhood friendship to the love that sacrifices itself without reservation for its friends, who ultimately are the whole human race! I would go even more deeply into the fullness of the created order were it not for the fact that only humans can respond in emotional and spiritual depth to one another. Thus it is far easier to love a pet whose means of response are strictly limited and who depends on its human master for its sustenance, than a fellow human whose ways are often devious, whose responses are frequently unpredictable, and whose loyalty can be like shifting sand before a desert wind. How wonderful it is, nevertheless, to communicate with a friend, unburdening oneself in trust to someone who knows the common passions and can listen with sympathy to one's problems and aspirations! To have even a few friends of this depth of commitment is a great achievement; one can judge the value of what one has given in one's life by the number of people whom one can in all humility number among one's friends. Friendship is cultivated by becoming a good friend oneself: to be sufficiently quiet to listen in attention to the other person is the way ahead, to lose oneself completely in that person's company is the moment when friendship is declared. One's life is bound to that of the other individual, and then one may be able to consider the self in its identification with the other, who is now one's friend. The friend's concern is for our happiness, and the essential criterion of this is the implicit trust in the relationship and the caring shown for our well-being.

Trust is the criterion of all real relationships. I am at my most trustworthy when I can throw myself open to the trust of my neighbour. The less I possess, the more open I can afford to be to those around me, for I have little to lose in the transaction. To become open to this degree, I have above all to lose concern for my image in the eyes of my fellows. Jesus says that it is hard for a man of wealth to enter the kingdom of God, easier indeed for a camel to go through the eye of a needle (Luke 18.24–25). Paradise is an atmosphere of such peace that we can enjoy each other's company in the glowing presence of God without any need of dissimulation or protection of our own imagined interests. As long as I am burdened by possessions that I feel obliged to guard at all costs and a personality which must be protected against all criticism, even from those people who have my true interests at heart, I cannot enter the peace of God's kingdom, the passport to which is complete childlike trust. This is indeed the faith that saves: accepting God's undemanding love, which the Christian would see as demonstrated incontestably in the sacrifice of Jesus for the whole world. He was the friend to all, even when they were incapable of reciprocating that friendship. There is only one reason why I should be accepted, and that is my origin in the divine mind and my creation by the divine love. When one remembers that origin and creation, one's personal attributes and possessions are seen as God's gifts to us that are to be used for the benefit of those around us. We are their stewards, not their owners, let alone their masters.

This understanding of the riches that life has granted us – and I speak of many more attributes than mere money, the particular commodity that prevented the rich man from entering heaven in the account to which I have already alluded (Luke 18.18–27) – gives them a finer significance. We are to take care of them in order to give freely to others, not as a duty laid down by spiritual counsel but as a great pleasure. To witness the faces of those who have been given food in their extremity of poverty is as moving as being among the audience at a really satisfying concert or play. All of these experiences lift us beyond the selfish gluttony of the market-place to the portals of heaven, where our common humanity is illuminated by rays of divine splendour. But we are no longer there merely as isolated spectators; we are part of a much greater whole in which we can begin to sense our full identity as part of the body of God. This is the body of Christ that the believer affirms during the course of the Eucharist. The gifts of God to us are therefore to be our way of participation in the Mass of life itself, where Christ is the eternal celebrant. 'Do you not know that your body is a temple of the indwelling Holy Spirit, and the Spirit is God's gift to you? You do not belong to yourselves; you were bought at a price. Then honour God in your body' (1 Corinthians 6.19–20). This fundamental teaching of St Paul is to be extended to all the gifts with which we have been endowed. Only then do they cease to be our private property and become instead the concern of the entire community. A responsibility of ownership is lifted from us as a joy of preservation falls to us in the company of all those around us. This is the way stewardship works within the caring community.

The emotion evoked by deep friendship is affection: there is a glowing warmth of affect that causes friends to embrace one another. Touch has often been evaded in human relationships as if it were invariably the portal of lust. This is very sad, because the touch of warm regard not only affirms the value of the other person's body (by which, after all, we all function while we are alive in the world) and therefore of themself as a whole person, but also has a healing quality when it is conferred in the sheer joy of recognition. The exchange of a sign of peace during the Eucharist is on this account to be welcomed, but in such a situation, when we greet stranger and friend alike, we have to take care that the embrace has a real quality of welcome and is not merely a ritual act. In this case the stranger is apt to be ignored after the service when the regular congregation meet for refreshment and conversation together. This common example shows the limitation of affection, no matter how enthusiastic it may be. It resembles the great affection the disciples had for their Master in the events leading up to his passion. They were quite sure that they were ready to give up their very lives for him, and there was no guile within the hearts of these simple working men. I suspect that it was for this quality that Jesus chose them for the very difficult assignment ahead of them during his death and the events that were to follow his resurrection and ascension, and the pouring down of the Holy Spirit upon them shortly afterwards. They had to learn that good intentions were not enough; indeed a popular proverb states that they pave the road to hell. Affection is a labile quality dependent largely on the attitude of the other person; if they, like Jesus, disappoint one, one soon becomes disillusioned, and rejection may follow in the wake. Peter's thrice repeated denial of Jesus is a terrible example of such a *volte-face*, though here it seems that fear rather than rejection lay at the heart of the disciples' attitude. As Jesus said of the three disciples who accompanied him to Gethsemane but could not keep awake while he was in agony, 'The spirit is willing, but the flesh is weak' (Mark 14.38).

Love, unlike affection, is not an emotion, though it nearly always is accompanied by an emotional response. Love is an action of the will whereby one gives of oneself that the other person may come fully into their own being as people fashioned in the image of God. On a more mundane level, the loving person cares for their friend under the guidance of God, not their own self-will. How can we be sure it is not our own will assuming a divine omniscience? By the dedication to the highest we may know, which is sacrifice and renunciation up to the submission to death itself if the situation demands it. The essential qualities of love are expressed in 1 John 4.16–21, crucially important statements among which are that God is love, and the person dwelling in love is dwelling in God. We love because of God's prior love for us. Perfect love banishes fear, because fear has punishment at its basis, while in love there is no room for such an attitude. Finally, our love for God is proved by the love we have for our fellows: we cannot love the invisible God while hating our fellow creatures. It must be admitted that in this passage the fellow creature is identified with a fellow Christian, but in the vastly more pluralistic world of the present time it is our duty to extend our love to all people, and to all that lives according to its nature and function in the world.

The type of loving situation that is highly emotional is the sexual experience of 'falling in love' with someone. The spiritual value of this emotional response lies in its effect in shifting the consciousness from ourself to another person, who, at least temporarily, becomes the centre of our thoughts and hopes to the extent that their absence is intolerable. Somehow we project all our desires on to this individual. If the response satisfies the test of time, it is right that a permanent union should be sought. Once such a union has been effected, the scales of self-imposed illusion rapidly drop from the eyes of the couple, and then follows the long journey to real self-giving love. The discipline of married life is much more valuable in this respect than a mere casual living together which can be terminated at any time according to the whim of one of the partners. The termination of marriage is nowadays very common in most countries, but a wise couple will see this as a positively final resort after all channels of reconciliation have been exhausted. We grow through conflict patiently borne; love emerges in the recesses of our souls when we have let God into the pain of the present situation, and then a new way is shown to us in coping with apparently irreconcilable incompatibilities: where there is a will, there is a way. Of course sometimes the way is clearly one of separation and divorce, and this too has to be faced with courage and as little rancour as possible. If we are wise, we thank God for all our experiences, even the nasty ones. They can, if properly accepted, form the basis of a kinder, more understanding type of person than we were when at the threshold of adult life. It is this person whom we take beyond death's portal to the mysterious world awaiting us.

Love is usually accompanied by strong affection, but sometimes it is neutral and even punitive. One may be sure that the father of the prodigal son was grievously upset by the way his foolish child took his money and left home without so much as a thought for his family. But the father did not interfere; he let his son get on with his own life, and did not even try to get in contact with him in an attempt to entice him to a more comfortable home. But when the prodigal came to himself, the father was ready to receive him with joy. His love had not grown sour, and was simply waiting for the return of the beloved. Numerous parents have had similar experiences in real life with children who have 'gone to the bad' with drugs, sexual promiscuity, occult involvement, and association with unpleasant cults that seek to seduce children from their families. They have learned to await events like the prodigal son's father, and not infrequently there has been a happy home-coming. On other occasions, it must be admitted, the outcome has been less fortunate, the children being permanently alienated from their own kind, but I believe the parents' caring has not been dulled. All this reminds us that we have no ownership of our offspring; we are their stewards as were Mary and Joseph when Jesus stayed behind in the temple at Jerusalem when he was twelve years old, oblivious of the consternation his absence was arousing among his relatives on the way back to their home in Nazareth after going to Jerusalem for the Passover (Luke 2.41–51).

'My son, do not spurn the Lord's correction or recoil from his reproof; for those whom the Lord loves he reproves, and he punishes a son who is dear to him' (Proverbs 3.11–12). This injunction emphasizes the sternness of love. It was seen especially dramatically in the story of Job. He was tested by Satan under the protecting presence of God; his trials were appalling, but he came through without blemish, and was privileged to see God as the supreme creator of all the wonders of the world. Compared with that understanding, all his suffering was a mere trifle, and the last part of his life had a placidity about it that was absent at the beginning of the story, when he was never quite sure of the degree of God's beneficence. Thus he felt impelled to make special sacrifices after his children's parties in case they had inadvertently made a blasphemous remark. If his trust had been perfect his love would have ensured that he had no such fear about divine retribution. It is when we have been deprived of those things that we regard as the very basis of our life that truth is given an opportunity to be heard, and then we may be silent with the divine presence and shown the way to personal transcendence. An obsessively clinging attitude to possessions and those whom we believe we love is the basis of our unhappiness. When we are able to let go we can at last relate in true love to our friends and relatives, for then they come to us as integral people who can give of their own essence to us, speaking the truth in love to both their and our benefit.

St Paul in his famous rhapsody on love in 1 Corinthians 13 stresses the patience and kindness of love (even when it is quite stern as in the consideration above). It does not envy other people, nor is it boastful, conceited, selfish, or hot-tempered in seeking its own justification. Thus it is not quick to take offence or to keep a score of grievances. It does not gloat over other people's sins, but always delights in the truth. Indeed there is no love where subterfuge prevails. Love can, on the contrary, face anything, and its faith, hope and endurance are limitless. Above all else it will never come to an end; this is surely the ultimate test of a person's love, as I am sure it typifies God's love towards his creatures. Some of us who are not conspicuously demonstrative in our emotional responses to other people are filled with love towards them; actions speak louder than words, as the saying goes. The emotion that bridges affection and love is compassion, the ability to enter into another being's suffering. The word 'being' brings in a greater range of concern than a merely human one, but I have no doubt that our first concern must be to our human fellows. If we truly love each other, that love is sure to overflow to all the creatures around us, and the same is true of the gentler compassion. On the other hand, there are some exponents of 'animal rights' who hate at least some of their fellow human beings. Love in fact is always universal in scope, since it comes from God and is the essential divine attribute. Inasmuch as God loves all his creatures, so does true human love have no limits. We can hardly help liking some people more than others, liking in this context having close affinities to affection, but we are bidden to love our enemies and pray for those who persecute us. Even people of low spiritual calibre may act lovingly to their friends and relatives (and even for this we should be grateful, for at least the attitude is right even if its scope is limited), but full love knows no favourites. Matthew 5.43–48 spells out these requirements of the godly life.

When we consider our poor showing in relation to these demands, we may feel very dispirited; the ideal is an immeasurable distance from our capacity. But then we should remember that God is the source of love and not we ourselves. Our great work is to become more open to the divine compassion, and then the love of God will pour into our souls. This openness is cultivated by the constant practice of silent prayer and a more balanced view of our frailties. A sense of humour is an invaluable adjunct, without which 'good' people become hard, censorious and painfully insensitive to the world's tragedies. What we can face without flinching, we can serve with compassion, and the first person for whom to have compassion is oneself. When we cease judging ourselves and can simply be still, a ripple of gentle humour can be allowed to play through ourself, and then we can entertain a smile at our deficiencies and start to love ourselves for what we are, not for our future achievements. It is in fact God's love for us that now becomes available to our own consciousness, and that love cannot be dammed within ourself as a selfish acquisition.

Love's nature is to circulate freely and initiate the act of creation, whether in living form or in a plenitude of mental or artistic inspiration. The more we can love ourselves, the more we begin to love our fellows and the world in general.

It must be admitted that the act of loving people whom we greatly dislike is not easy; Jesus, for that matter, did not like many of the scribes and Pharisees whom he met in the course of his work. Furthermore, love does not flourish in an atmosphere of deception; we must maintain the truth in a spirit of love (Ephesians 4.15). There are unfortunately some people with whom nearly everybody has a difficulty in relating; the unanimity of response exonerates our own dislike. Such people will remain outsiders until they are prepared to investigate their own psychological condition. Usually they are either very obtuse or very proud, often both together, and nothing can be done to relate better with them. But one can still care about them in prayer, while awaiting a change in heart in their lives. If the matter is one of a more personal vendetta, it is right to try and bring the situation to an open discussion. Often this is impossible because of the intractable disposition of the other person. In the end the wisest and best way is that of forgiveness, so that one may devote one's attentions to one's own affairs rather than dissipating them on evil thoughts and obsessive plans for revenge. Wisdom may be provided by a kindly friend: what was lost, whether a spouse in the course of infidelity or money through dishonesty, can be replaced if one sets one's mind squarely to the matter. In respect of infidelity, the spouse has exposed themself as inadequate in any case, while the experience of financial loss can be of great future value in the course of one's life. Needless to say, a criminal offence should be brought to the notice of the law, as much for the offender's ultimate good as for the welfare of society. A failure to do so is an act of sentimentality, not of love. We remember the strong dictum of Proverbs 3.11–12 once more, to the effect that we should not spurn God's reproof and correction, for God loves those whom he reproves, even punishing a son who is dear to him. Inasmuch as we are all God's beloved children, we must accept punishment when we clearly go off the rails.

The heart of the matter is the experience that life provides the open-hearted type of person: we all start as self-centred children, but as we work in the world, so we can appreciate other types of people with tastes other than our own. These include religious belief (or unbelief), national allegiance, life style, political commitment and artistic appreciation. Some of these categories may remain closed books to us, while others are the very life of the spirit within us. As we grow older, an overriding wisdom should direct our attention, seeing all the above categories as essentially focuses of personal growth. Our opinions are certain to change with the advent of age and its concomitant experience of the nature of people and society. What ought to grow even as the body declines is compassion for all life, so that our concern may be the fruit of deep commitment to the sufferings of our fellows, and a determination to relieve their pain as much as possible. This is the apogee of love, and if we have actualized it for even one person, we need not be ashamed of our contribution to the whole. 'Anything you did for one of my brothers here, however insignificant, you did for me' (Matthew 25.40). We have noted this dictum before.

To continue giving oneself in love to a person who cannot respond is a great test of relationship. How can one continue to take a real interest in a spouse who is languishing in hospital in the last stages of Alzheimer's disease, when the rational response is so minimal that it is extremely doubtful whether the patient even recognizes their visitor? One has always to be honest in one's reactions; play-acting simply increases the sense of ultimate alienation. I believe that when the brain is so damaged by the degenerative changes of Alzheimer's disease or the frank destruction of tissue that follows a stroke or an injury, the essential being of a person may be intact but unable to communicate intelligibly through an irremediably damaged brain, the master organ of the body that controls all responses while we are alive in the flesh. If one considers this possibility one may still address the person with the hope that there is a deeper recognition even if the response is negligible. True love embraces the entire person and looks for no response to justify it.

A similar attitude should inform us in our relationship with a chronically mentally ill person, but here the hope of amelioration is often quite strong. There have been instances of victims of manic-depressive psychosis who so irritated their spouse during a hypomanic phase with its hyperactivity and loquacity that they were bidden to keep quiet rather brusquely by their exhausted partner. All did indeed become quiet, but the person was found hanged elsewhere in the house! How careful we have to be in dealing with the mentally ill! True love can bear all things, but can one dare blame the husband or wife vexed almost beyond control, especially when the psychosis has been continuing for a long time? Needless to say, the sense of guilt that hangs over the spouse whose impatience has precipitated the insane suicidal act is worsened by the love the two shared during periods of lucidity and living together. The lesson to be learned from this is to practise self-control and be quiet within oneself even when one is provoked to breaking point. In that quietness the love of God can soften and warm the tense heart; a tragedy is averted as one grows more fully into the serenity of a holy person, something of the measure of fullness of the stature of Christ.

George Herbert's glorious poem on love seems to say everything about the subject.

Love bade me welcome; yet my soul drew back,
Guilty of dust and sin.
But quick-eyed Love, observing me grow slack
From my first entrance in,
Drew nearer to me, sweetly questioning
If I lack'd anything.

'A guest,' I answer'd, 'worthy to be here:'
Love said, 'You shall be he.'
'I, the unkind, ungrateful? Ah, my dear,
I cannot look on thee.'
Love took my hand, and smiling did reply,
'Who made the eyes but I?'

'Truth, Lord; but I have marr'd them: let my shame
Go where it doth deserve.'
'And know you not,' says Love, 'who bore the blame?'
'My dear, then I will serve.'

'You must sit down,' says Love, 'and taste my meat:'
So I did sit and eat.

And yet Shakespeare still has something more personal to add in one of his sonnets.

Let me not to the marriage of true minds
Admit impediments. Love is not love
Which alters when it alteration finds,
Or bends with the remover to remove:
O, no! It is an ever-fixèd mark,
That looks on tempests and is never shaken;
It is the star to every wand'ring bark,
Whose worth's unknown, although his height be taken.
Love's not Time's fool, though rosy lips and cheeks
Within his bending sickle's compass come;
Love alters not with his brief hours and weeks,
But bears it out even to the edge of doom: –
If this be error and upon me proved,
I never writ, nor no man ever loved.

Yes indeed, charity never faileth, to quote the Authorized Version's lovely rendering of 1 Corinthians 13.8. Love will never come to an end, in the words of the Revised English Bible.

8 The sense of the ridiculous

I find no book in the Bible more refreshing than Ecclesiastes. It is a peak of the Wisdom literature of Israel, and was probably written in the third century BC, some seven centuries after the time of King Solomon to whom tradition ascribes both this book and Proverbs. The joy of Ecclesiastes depends paradoxically on its sour dictum and generally pessimistic conclusions. Worldly success frequently bears no relationship to the character of the person who attains high office; the same applies to the attainment of riches. And even wealth does not assure one of anything other than anxiety. 'Sweet is the sleep of a labourer whether he has little or much to eat, but the rich man who has too much cannot sleep' (5.12). The reason for this insomnia is twofold: the obvious anxiety about the safety of one's possessions, and the rich, excessive and generally unhealthy meals that the affluent are accustomed to eat. At first this is a mark of their elevation in human eyes, but soon it becomes a thoughtless habit to be reciprocated by and on their kind at various parties and civic functions. How fortunate are those who can live with an ardent spirit controlling the needs of the body! If, however, one's concerns are primarily mundane, the spirit has little to do except enjoin a degree of prudence in the face of immediate desire and seduction. The labourer's sleep is, according to the above dictum, sweet only if contentment blesses his efforts. The pleasantly bucolic atmosphere conjured up by Ecclesiastes is less in evidence in our contemporary world where most people are imbued with a spirit of worldly ambition, each wishing to make the grade and be free of financial hardship. Then they too can enjoy the 'good things of life', see the sights, and vie with their peers in acquiring a superficial knowledge about many things in general but little in particular.

Someone very close to me used to make it his business to visit as many of the great sights of the world as he could. He did not believe in a life beyond death, and his dictum was 'Once you're dead, you're dead for a long time'. I learned to smile indulgently rather than to involve myself in a heated discussion with him, knowing full well that the evidence for survival of death is a very personal matter. He is in fact now dead to his physical body, but I have had a number of very personal communications from his soul, or 'spirit', all initiated directly by him (for I do not patronize mediums except very rarely, and then for the purpose of psychical research). He now knows that there is indeed something awaiting the deceased in the life beyond death, and I suspect feels that his feverish attempts to see as much as possible of this world before his death were rather pathetic and self-centred.

The burden of the teaching of the unknown writer of Ecclesiastes is that all earthly striving is in vain. 'Swiftness does not win the race nor strength the battle. Food does not belong to the wise, nor wealth to the intelligent, nor success to the skilful; time and chance govern all' (9.11). No one knows when the hour of tragedy or death may strike, and indeed it is far wiser not to know the exact time of these inevitable occurrences, because in the end little can be done about them, while a neurotic preparation for them will only rob the present moment of its innocent joys and happy expectations. It is in this respect that we can agree with Thomas Gray's rather trite observation from his 'Ode on a Distant Prospect of Eton College', 'Where ignorance is bliss, 'tis folly to be wise'. Wisdom, or at least knowledge, may be useful if it can reverse an unpleasant situation in time, but there are many events in our life that are not tractable to interference of this type, and if we are truly wise we learn to live with them, accept them, and grow through them to become more adult members of society. Jesus also says in the course of the Sermon the Mount, 'Do not be anxious about tomorrow; tomorrow will look after itself. Each day has troubles enough of its own' (Matthew 6.34).

The end of all earthly life, whether human or animal, whether of kings or commoners, of saints or sinners, of self-assured religionists or agnostics, is dissolution of the body and a return of the spirit to God who gave it (Ecclesiastes 12.7). Indeed, everything mortal is futile, vain and illusory if seen in an isolated, selfish context. But we were never expected to live thus. We are expected to enrich the world from which we spring, and to work in the company of all our fellows, whether in direct fellowship or in the more vastly ranging compass of prayer. We enrich the world by giving our own special essence to it; a depressive type of person can see nothing valuable about himself or herself, whereas a self-assured individual may have an absurdly exaggerated opinion of his or her own importance. We are most helpful to the community when we forget ourselves and proceed with the work at hand. If we are a relatively undistinguished member of a group there will probably be more competent members to complement our endeavours. In fact the especially gifted person shines most beautifully when they serve in a selfless enthusiasm in a communal enterprise. This type of person, if they are imbued with a spontaneous humility that is a distant promise of greatness, is so concerned about the other members as to be scarcely aware of the special contribution they are making. They lose themself only to discover their true identity in the context of the fullness of the group.

It is ironic that the depressed individual is so encumbered by a broken self-image that there is no possibility of them participating in the great company of living compatriots. On the other hand, the self-assured egoist excludes themself by an inflating, often narcissistic display that estranges the other members of the company with whom they labour. Jesus warns such an egoist to watch their step: they may select a place of honour at a wedding feast, only to be demoted when a more auspicious guest arrives; it is far better to take a lowly place and then be invited by the host up higher. Furthermore, all the other guests will note the respect with which these favoured ones are held (Luke 14.7–11). The ridiculous aspect of us humans is the way we get our sense of proportion completely out of balance. Our moods are at their most laughably exalted when we believe that we amount to something special or that our opinions are of special worth when we compare ourselves with our peers. Our undeniable particularity lies in the essence of the soul, or true self, but it is in no way to be inflated above the souls of others around us. Some of us actualize our gifts and talents, like the servants described in Jesus' famous parable of Matthew 25.14–30, whereas many more go to sleep as life passes them unobtrusively by. It is a commonplace among all the world's great spiritual teachers that most people function as sleepwalkers. Some of the more arrogant of their followers prescribe special exercises or work to counteract this unawareness, but to those with greater spiritual insight, all that is stimulated is an egoistic concern that obliterates the finer feelings that lead to loving service.

In this respect not all service has a loving quality. Apart from the service demanded by a tyrannical overlord in a servile relationship, there is a kind of service exacted from the pupil by a masterful teacher. This type of situation is not uncommon in many of the cults at present captivating the young in their search for an absolute truth which they have failed to obtain in the world's religious traditions. Not only do the seekers after truth give their very souls to their masterful (and predatory) teachers, but they also submit themselves to incredibly exacting service in the cause of the cult. One might add that the true teachers of spiritual truth never demand anything personal of their students even if they demand the whole world from them, as Jesus did of the rich young man who sought to attain eternal life. He advised him to relinquish his money, which was the focus of anchorage to transience and worldly illusion, but this was to go to the poor, not to Jesus and his little company. At that stage of his life the postulant found it impossible to comply with Jesus' invitation to absolute renunciation and then to follow him (Mark 10.17–22). There is a fine honesty about this man and the teacher completely absent in the modern cult situation: the seeker has a grasping attitude to what he or she believes is the truth, while the alleged master grasps the pupil and their belongings without any scruple whatsoever. Here we have a nice example of the ridiculous at play in the tragic human situation: it is the spiritually blind who lead those with at least partial sight, sufficient to drive them onwards to seek the truth. Their contact with the blind man leads to their own progressive blindness, but it is at least remediable when, like the prodigal son, they come to their senses and hear the voice of God the Holy Spirit within them. It is interesting to compare this travesty of truth and service with the real thing as described in Jesus' restoration of sight to the man born blind in the ninth chapter of St John's gospel.

Jesus warns us that we cannot serve God and Mammon, the god of money (Luke 16.13). But money can have a far wider context than merely its wonted usage as a convenient medium of exchange; in its entirety it embraces all the things of the world, which are mere idols when served in their own capacity to the exclusion of any higher concern. The ego can be the most seductive of all idols, for it unconsciously forms the basis of an extreme form of worship. Paradoxically enough, this is true of the depressive situation, but here it is the hiatus formed by the virtually obliterated ego that forms the basis of self-awareness, so that the victim is tied to a non-existence that is the very foundation of their identity. More usually the ego is challengingly dominant and looks for its own satisfaction above all else. It often assumes a religious flavour, on other occasions a political or nationalistic one. And so it comes about that these and kindred matters may form the essence of our lives to the extent of our trying to silence dissenters in defence of what we regard as the truth, but what is in fact merely our own opinion. The ego is a most serviceable garment of the soul, but if we are defective in spiritual insight we may be deceived into focusing our full attention on to it, so as to avoid those deeper issues in the psyche which relate to our identity. The fear we experience when this part of the personality is threatened by exposure can be truly paralysing, because we are confronted with conflict and possible destruction.

The Psalmist marvels at God's creation of the human in Psalm 8, where he is described as little less than a god (verse 5). But he can also function as a mass destroyer when he believes he has a divine mission, sent in fact by his coruscating ego rather than the Spirit within, which shines with the uncreated light of God as it illuminates the soul and inflames the whole person with a love that will give of itself without stint for the benefit of the whole, whether of the group, the nation or all that lives. In the light of love all of these coalesce to form what we may reasonably call the body of Christ. The uncreated light of God, the energy by which we know the presence of the Almighty – for of God no one can speak except in negative terms, of what is not rather than of what is – is at once blinding and illuminating, searing and healing, revealing and supporting. The light of the demon-possessed individual with a yearning for absolute power consuming their soul is alluring and scintillating, its strength magnifying itself and deceiving its object so that its source lies unrevealed except to those of spiritual sight who can discern the emptiness of the chalice from which it emanates. This falsified light also comes primarily from God, who is the source of all life, power and light, but it is shown to be perverted by the corrupted will of the creature who has grasped at a divine status.

The cleansing power that restores the human to something of the divine image in which they were created is contained in two little esteemed qualities of common life: doubt and humour. The person who can truly accept the glaring possibility that their convictions, so dearly and loyally held, may be, if not frankly erroneous, at least needful of modification and constant audit, is in a state of grace; the grace of God is capable of penetrating the skin of their certainty with a love that supersedes any necessity for absolute correctness that may assume the plausible mask of truth. Doubt is something illustrated in Thomas's refusal to accept the verity of Jesus' resurrected form until he had direct evidence of the marks of his crucifixion. When these were shown, his faith was absolute (John 20.26–29). Doubt reveals the tentative nature of all worldly phenomena and beliefs. It is our growing point into a fresh understanding of reality, and will never cease until the end of time itself. 'At present we see only puzzling reflections in a mirror, but one day we shall see face to face. My knowledge now is partial; then it will be whole, like God's knowledge of me' (1 Corinthians 13.12). But the passage is completed by the crucial observation that only three things last forever, and these are faith, hope and the greatest of the three, love. This everlasting faith is a most important quality to investigate, and I shall do this later. But the sort of faith that has an intellectual, credal basis is at most merely a summation of current understanding, easily taken over by prejudice that masquerades as the truth. It is this sort of faith, whether religious, philosophical or political, that is the basis of conflict to death. Once one can let go and accept that other people with contrary beliefs may also have some truth, and that the wise person listens with respect to all and sundry, just as Jesus did when he dined with the less reputable members of society and entered fully into their conviviality, one can grow in understanding of the human condition and be of immense help to others who are in difficulty. (If he had been 'standoffish' because of moral disapproval, he would never have been asked a second time either to that particular group or to any others, because his reputation would quickly have spread by word of mouth.)

If all real living is meeting, to quote Buber a third time, we increase our knowledge by social intercourse in a way that books and lectures can never match. Jesus not only learned the wisdom of the streets – if he were alive today the inmates of our prisons would have enlightened him about many less acceptable aspects of society as well as their own particular psychological gifts and problems – but also the heroism of the common folk living in subservience to the Romans, their own traitorous tax-gatherers and the general state of poor hygiene that caused many people to die at least as young as he himself. We often forget that as little as a century ago many people in western Europe died before the age of forty from infections that are nowadays easily treated by antibiotics; AIDS, however, reminds us that nature has unpleasant tricks 'up its sleeve' until we participate in spiritual as well as intellectual maturity.

Doubt is an amazing liberator; it frees us for more research, whether social, scientific or personal. While some people need scriptural literalism, often called fundamentalism, to make them feel secure, there are others who are able to outgrow such reins on the intelligence. They are the pioneers of the race. Some will certainly die in unfortunate circumstances, for the experiment of life, like all other experiments, is hazardous, but at least they will have actualized their true humanity, will never be satisfied until the ultimate truth has been revealed, the ultimate exploration attempted. In the end they are to discover that all ultimate things are spiritual rather than merely material and intellectual, and then a faith comes to them that is of a very different quality from a dependence on dogmas of various types that enslave rather than enlighten. It is not that dogmas and teachings are *ipso facto* erroneous, but that they tend in the wrong hands to promote a dogmatism which will not relent until it has placed as many people as possible under its thraldom. Modern scientific practice is expanding so fast that all teachings have a transient quality about them, but religious consciousness, being less easily tested, tends to embrace definite schemes of thought that either do not move or else are tentatively replaced by equally dogmatic ideas that induce an illusion of absolute authority. It is very refreshing to encounter a person of intelligent, sympathetic doubt who can appreciate the enduring features of the old way without being subservient to them; an iconoclastic attitude is seldom helpful to an individual's growth or the community's development.

Doubt above all else shows us how foolish we are when we become wedded to concepts, theories or philosophies. If we have a sense of proportion we can scarcely suppress a smile when we think about some of the beliefs that have guided human thought over past eras. They have concerned the assurance that various religious and metaphysical dogmas have been God's will. In a more sober frame of mind can we really believe that a God of love will condemn even a very hardened sinner to eternal damnation, an irreversible hell from which that love is totally excluded? Since God is the ultimate creator of all that exists, would he have devised such an atmosphere of torment that knows of no relief? One must concede that some of Jesus' parables, notably those of Matthew 25 and Luke 16.19–31, envisage such a condition of total unforgiveness, despite Jesus' own reputation for love and forgiveness. Depending on one's own insights one will accept or reject such a final disposal of one's fellow beings, but if one is wise one will wonder who exactly is to share such a terrible fate. Why not oneself? The more one grows spiritually, the more unworthy does one see oneself, and the deficiency is always one of love. When all is considered it is much more likely that a hell of unlimited duration may be the outlook for the vicious sinner until the expression of repentance, rather like that of the prodigal son returning home to his father after a long period in the hell that he had improvidently devised for himself. Thus intelligent doubt can modify longstanding beliefs without necessarily rejecting them altogether.

The sense of the ridiculous in human life is exposed most perfectly by the humour of the present moment. Life, far from being solemn, is one glorious laugh when we are fully aware of what is laid before us, however serious the present situation may be. Recently when I was conducting a few days' silent retreat of serious intent – though not too severe, I hope – a trivial incident occurred during our silent lunch together while I sat at table with two other retreatants. At the end of the meal we were served with the dessert consisting of boiled rhubarb with some custard contained in a small jug. As I started pouring the custard on to the rhubarb, I failed to observe that there was an obstruction which caused me to tilt the jug more acutely; it then became obvious that the obstruction was caused by a small piece of clotted custard blocking the lip of the jug. Once this little clot had been detached there was a considerable flow of custard on to my plate. This little diversion evoked a giggle in us all which broadened into a delicious smile. The lady next to me then started sprinkling sugar on her rhubarb, but she too had a minor mishap: the top of the sprinkler was poorly attached and became loose, with the result that an unusually heavy flow of sugar coated her dessert. It was the incongruous little episode from common life amid the concentrated silence that sparked off our amusement. Had a similar event occurred in a domestic setting it would either have passed without comment or else occasioned mild irritation. In an expensive restaurant there might have been some annoyance, except that boiled rhubarb would have been a distinctly unlikely dessert in a classy eating-house! From this very simple example we can see how humour is closely integrated into our common life at any time provided we have the awareness and simplicity to appreciate it. It casts its ridicule over all our pretensions without in any way discrediting our endeavours. There is, on the contrary, something very endearing about a humorous event: we seem somehow to be taken up in the everlasting arms of God, being assured that God is love, and that in the love our mighty schemes and dogmatic points of view can be put to rest for a little while.

To laugh at oneself is the apogee of humour. To see our foibles in the light of a charitable openness and to smile indulgently over them is a mark of distinct spiritual development. Such an attitude softens our wonted rigidity, and allows us to love both ourself and other people for what we all are, rather as God does. I thank God for the ministry of humorists, comedians and clowns. By their outrageous assaults on the apparent normality of everyday life, they cause me to draw breath, and in that action I draw in something of the mystery of God also. When I lose rigid control of my own propriety, I attain an openness to vast ranges of emotion that put me in touch with the human condition at its most child-like. Can one find humour in the Bible? If one reads it straight through with a single-track mind, looking for infallible teaching or filled with adoration, one will see nothing of the texture of humour, simply because one has unwittingly blinded oneself to the full text.

When I was a child I used to love the story of Job, whose depth I could scarcely fathom at that age, but the wording of the Authorized Version delighted me: 'Behold now behemoth, which I made with thee; he eateth grass as an ox . . . ', and 'Canst thou draw out leviathan with an hook? Or his tongue with a cord which thou lettest down? Canst thou put an hook into his nose? Or bore his jaw through with a thorn? Will he make many supplications unto thee? Will he speak soft words to thee? Will he make a covenant with thee?' And so the delightful descriptions of the hippopotamus and the crocodile proceed in Job 40 and 41 respectively. I doubt whether I could have identified behemoth and leviathan when I was a child, but the pleasure they gave me was out of this world in sheer enjoyment. And then there was the story of the death of the wicked king of Israel, Ahab, who was directed by Jehoshaphat to find a reliable prophet to foretell their joint venture in the battle of Ramoth-gilead against the Syrians. 'And Jehoshaphat said, Is there not a prophet of the Lord besides [the numerous prophets who unanimously forecast victory], that we may enquire of him? And the king of Israel said unto Jehoshaphat, There is yet one man, Micaiah the son of Imlah, by whom we may enquire of the Lord, but I hate him; for he doth not prophesy good concerning me, but evil' (1 Kings 22.7–8). The story in its delightful language goes on to tell of how Micaiah does indeed foretell disaster, which is soon accomplished. None of this is particularly amusing to the person devoid of a sense of humour, but if one does possess this invaluable gift, one can smile at the folly of Ahab in believing that he can alter the pre-ordained course of history by selecting the right type of prophet, one who gives him the type of counsel that will confirm his plans. We have already considered the problem of predestination and free will in Chapter 3; it is when we, like Jonah, strive to thwart our destiny that the fun begins. Those with a sense of humour can attain a balance that obviates foolish excursions into unknown territory in order to escape the nemesis in front of us, rather like Balaam and his ass who is gifted with a clairvoyance denied its owner (Numbers 22.24–25).

I find considerable source of humour in the Old Testament, but scarcely any in the New Testament. This is because there is much less delineation of character in this part of the Bible. The only slightly comical person is Peter, who vacillates between a moving loyalty to his Master (John 6.68–69) and a craven denial of his relationship (John 18.25–27). He can hardly believe that with Jesus' support he can walk on water, and then he begins to sink (Matthew 14.29–31), and with James and John he is privileged to witness the Transfiguration, the raising of the daughter of Jairus and the Gethsemane episode. In none of these three is there any evidence that he understands what is taking place. I can identify myself with Peter very easily in his fallible humanity, but whether I possess his strong loyalty – despite the 'hiccup' mentioned above – is something yet to be proved in its entirety. There is something to smile at in Paul's dogmatic views on church order: he sometimes closes a discussion by telling his readers that this is the way, and they must take it or leave it; nevertheless he believes that with a greater consideration over the matter in question they will come to see the truth of his own position! Considering the circumstances in which Paul did his tremendous missionary work

85

we are wise to applaud his efforts, even if he did cause some unhappiness among his Corinthian flock, but nowadays such a masterful approach will not attract the more thoughtful type of person whom the Church needs desperately in its current missionary activities.

If we have a strong sense of humour we allow for differences in opinion, welcoming criticism rather than regarding it as a manifestation of disloyalty. If we return where we started, to Ecclesiastes, everything ends in death, 'For mortals depart to their everlasting home, and the mourners go about the street' (12.5). It is wise not to take the world's enthusiasms and aversions too much to heart; what was taboo yesterday becomes the done thing today. What will happen tomorrow God alone knows. It is sure to be something that we in our self-assurance never so much as expected. Nevertheless, to quote 1 Corinthians 13.13 again, 'There are three things that last for ever: faith, hope, and love; and the greatest of the three is love'.

Humour is seen most exquisitely in little things. The episode at the retreat house is a typical example. Joy trickles down our faces as we laugh over the small times of cheerful abandon when we forget ourselves. It is then that we find ourselves as part of an infinitely greater whole than we could have imagined. In this way humour has a strongly mystical element. William Blake knew this in his exquisitely simple poem 'Laughing Song' which comes from the *Songs of Innocence*.

When the green woods laugh with the voice of joy
And the dimpling stream runs laughing by,
When the air does laugh with our merry wit,
And the green hill laughs with the noise of it.

When the meadows laugh with lively green
And the grasshopper laughs in the merry scene,
When Mary and Susan and Emily,
With their sweet round mouths sing Ha, Ha, He.

When the painted birds laugh in the shade
Where our table with cherries and nuts is spread
Come live & be merry and join with me,
To sing the sweet chorus of Ha, Ha, He.

A much more ridiculous element is found in the light operas of W. S. Gilbert and Arthur Sullivan and the nonsense poems of Edward Lear:

The Owl and the Pussy-Cat went to sea
In a beautiful pea-green boat.
They took some honey, and plenty of money,
Wrapped up in a five-pound note.
The Owl looked up to the Stars above
And sang to a small guitar,
'O lovely Pussy! O Pussy my love,
What a beautiful Pussy you are,
   You are,
   You are,
What a beautiful Pussy you are!'

Pussy said to the Owl, 'You elegant fowl!
How charmingly sweet you sing!
O let us be married! too long we have tarried:
But what shall we do for a ring?'
They sailed away for a year and a day,
To the land where the Bong-tree grows,
And there in a wood a Piggy-wig stood
With a ring at the end of his nose.
   His nose,
   His nose,
With a ring at the end of his nose.

A sense of humour is innate. It is incompatible with fanaticism and is needed to subdue intense partisan feelings about religion and politics. It is developed during periods of stress; tragedy paradoxically often leads to its flowering. It is not surprising that the Jews and the Irish, two groups with a particularly sad history, are renowned for their fund of arresting jokes and especially their humorous attitude to life itself. My own sense of humour, always very pronounced, was well brought out during my years as a morbid anatomist, a pathologist who specializes in post-mortem examinations, among other interests. The aesthetically repulsive atmosphere of the mortuary where autopsies are performed soon precipitates a subtle change of attitude, in the course of which one converses jocularly with the post-mortem attendant, both being involved in a work of distinctly unusual fascination. One thinks of cremations with a fee attached and inquests that are even more lucrative. The amount of money provided by either was in fact negligible, but the thought of getting something lifted one's imagination to the pleasant reward in store for one at the end of the day. Distinctly irreverent banter might escape from one's lips, and the ridiculous futility of so much mortal pretension was unmasked in the ritual of the post-mortem room. But there were moments of great sadness also, as when a young person had died. I look back on that period of my life with almost unbearable nostalgia, revolting as it may have been from a purely aesthetic point of view. But the keen sense of humour has persisted and been augmented by the folly one sees so often in one's own actions and in the pomposity of those who feel they have a special gift to show, rather than share with, their fellows.

9 Desolation and its aftermath

We experience desolation when the very bottom of our private world is removed from under us. The bottom seems to be pulled away, and in its place there is left a terrifying void which cannot be filled by either our own efforts or the concern of our friends. This brings us to the crucial question, 'On what do we depend most in our lives?' If we are loyal members of a religious body, we may confidently answer 'God', or 'Christ', or the founder of some other religious faith. But what is God? We inevitably couch God in anthropomorphic symbols, tending, for instance to use a gender (usually masculine), and we unthinkingly make this artifact contingent on our own desires and opinions. It is all too easy to fashion a god in our own image, which we then start to worship quite devoutly. Those who affirm an agnostic or atheistic position will admit to depending on intimate personal relationships, or possessions, or their place in the contemporary scene. When the rich young man came to Jesus to find out how he might attain eternal life, he was advised to sell everything he had and give the proceeds to the poor. At that stage in his life the rich man could not make that renunciation of his own free will, but it may be that later he was better prepared to let go of the single earthly bond that stood in the way of a full relationship with God.

It is no easy matter to relinquish something very dear to us, but until we do we can never know freedom. In between the loss and the greater life ahead yawns the chasm of desolation. We may do all we can to avoid it, but we may be quite sure that it will remain to confront us, often when we least expect it. It is a fact that desolation is a necessary experience for the person on the road to self-mastery. The reward is such a real knowledge of God that anthropomorphic images may be left behind. This God will never desert one because a presence of aspiration informs all time and space, creating a realm of uncreated light by which all things are made. This light may be identified with Christ, but just as we grope for the essential Christ amid the chaos of human claims and assertions, so we remain ignorant of God until we have lost ourself in the gaping void of the present moment. It is no wonder that the rich man chose to stay with his wealth and leave the demanding company of Jesus and his distinctly unprepossessing little band of disciples! It is always safer to stay with the known than to venture into the unknown.

Life, however, does not treat us in this comfortable way. We are, like the man whom Jesus healed after thirty-eight years of paralysis, urged to take up our bed and walk (John 5.1–9). Sometimes desolation follows a removal of some object around which our life revolved, and then its course can be clearly charted, but there are occasions when our sore is beyond healing and we have to prepare for a new life, sometimes in this world and sometimes in the world beyond death. But whatever we may feel when we are desolate, one thing is certain: we are on the move rather like the Israelites on their exodus towards the Holy Land. Not infrequently they yearned for the prison that was Egypt when things seemed to be going wrong for them in the long journey through the wilderness, but they had to go on. Fortunately for them their leader Moses under the guidance and providence of God was able to supply their needs. They eventually became more civilized, and were able at least to glimpse a finer way ahead even if they could not stay the course for long. This was the basic history of the Israelites up to the destruction of Jerusalem and the Temple in 587 BC; when a band of exiles from Babylon returned some sixty years later they had learned what obedience to God really meant, and their religion became more inward and spiritual even though the Temple was rebuilt. The desolation that followed the Babylonian destruction was fructified in the emergence of a new conception of religion that stemmed from Moses and the great prophets, but was now at least in part capable of being practised in everyday life.

When we lose something irreplaceable, at least in the short term, we enter the well-recorded experience of bereavement. Its most harrowing anguish accompanies the death of a loved one, but the desolation of loss can follow the disappointment of our dearest hopes in any sphere of endeavour. And here we move to the heart of desolation: the removal of hope. Chapter 6 was devoted to the hope that does not pale, but what about the hope that seems irrevocably smashed, so that disaster, failure and the unbearable emptiness of an unfulfilled life is all that is left to us? The experience is one of a total void far worse than any concept of death that we may have. After all, to the agnostic death is only like a dreamless sleep that bears of no awakening, a general anaesthetic that is destined to continue for ever. But the void of desolation is terrifyingly alive: every function of the body is retarded yet makes its pain of dysfunction miserably felt, so that no physical discomfort is allayed, no mental pain softened, no spiritual disillusionment disproved. There is also an obscure but very real feeling of shame, so that one does not wish to show oneself in public. All this, of course, shows how wrongly our self-image is set. We enjoy presenting ourselves to the world as well-set, successful people, success being interpreted as an abundance of the commodities that the prince of the world, alias Satan, teaches us to hold dear. It is not the commodities that are wrong so much as our attitude to them; desire makes us their prisoners. It is strangely ironical that in the phase of desolation we are set free from the meretricious values of the world. This is indeed our personal *via dolorosa*, and we are making the well-tried journey to our own particular cross. All those around Jesus were filled with a mixture of horror and contempt. We imagine that mixture in all those whom we meet, even sometimes those whom we regarded as our friends, but the attitude of rejection lies much more in us than in them. It must also be said that most people's memory is short-lived, provided the matter does not impinge too squarely on themselves or their families. Therefore there are few on whom we can depend. 'Put no trust in princes or in any mortal, for they have no power to save. When they breathe their last breath, they return to the dust, and on that day their plans come to nothing' (Psalm 146.3–4).

This is certainly the universal end of all humans. What we want on a personal level is essentially illusory. At the most the fulfilment of our plans gives us temporary pleasure, unless our lives have truly been dedicated to the loving service of our fellow creatures; in that service we lose ourselves and find our renewed self in the faces of all those for whom we have striven. The person in their little hell of desolation is beginning to learn the way of discrimination between the transitory and the permanent, between the egoistical and the universal. In our time of desolation we are peculiarly alone, because our sensitivity to human contact can be almost unbearable. Any kindly gesture is easily misconstrued as pity, a most unbecoming and even dangerous emotion. On the surface it is merely a feeling of tenderness to someone who is in distress, but deeper down there is also an attitude of regret, of feeling sorry, for the person as well. One feels distinctly superior and slightly judgemental as well. One feels one ought to do something to help, but from the position of being able to distribute one's largesse to someone inferior to oneself. This type of 'duty' is unconsciously demeaning to the afflicted individual. No wonder that person tends to shy away from all such dutiful help, and in their extreme emotional sensitivity they tend to see all assistance in this objectionable light. Pity can become dangerous when the desolate person accepts the help of the dutiful one at face value, and then, if he or she begins to depend increasingly on the assistance of the benefactor, a state of tension can develop in which the relationship between the two eventually becomes fraught to the point of an explosion. The benefactor feels that too great a demand is being made on their generosity, while the victim becomes increasingly disillusioned and bitter. Compassion, which is mentioned in Chapter 7, is of quite another order; here there is an identification with the sufferer so that one shares their affliction. One knows intuitively that the only help one can give – apart from material assistance where this is urgently required – is communicative silence. There is an immense support in this, for all our deepest emotions are laid to at least a temporary rest in the silence of the present moment.

Desolation is relieved in fitful sleep, but eventually the person wins through after a variable period of pain, especially if assisted by sensitive and knowledgeable friends. As one emerges from the incommunicable hell of desolation, one is encouraged inwardly by a promise of a future where one can function in buoyant self-esteem. This is how hope breaks into a mood of black dereliction: the inner being both lightens and expands, so that it seems to reach out to the light and draw that light into itself. This light is the uncreated light of God, though in this stage of expression it is felt in the heart rather than seen by the eye of the soul, as in the height of mystical illumination. It sounds absurd to speak of a light that is felt rather than seen, but the point of contact is the warmth that makes one glow in a fresh vision of further existence where one has reached beyond the old life to something startlingly new. To endeavour to describe inner emotional states is scarcely possible except to the person who has passed beyond the limitations of purely rational sensation to the inner world of feeling and intuition – returning to the four personality functions of sensation, feeling, thinking and intuition that we considered in Chapter 5.

There is some desolation that is not relieved as easily as this. It goes on, and any point of hope assumes the nature of a frank illusion. No one who deals with patients suffering from motor neurone disease or inoperable cancer can escape this experience albeit as an observer rather than a sufferer – when the victim is a loved one, the observer suffers at least as acutely as the beloved. An especially harrowing example is contained in the passion of Christ. First there is the preliminary horror of Gethsemane, when in the agony of suffering Jesus asks that, since all things are possible for the Father, the cup may be removed from him, yet according to the Father's will and not his own (Mark 14.36). The nature of this incommunicable suffering is obscure. One suggestion is the imminence of death, from which Jesus, like any other mortal, shrinks. I think that in addition to this, Jesus was assailed by the evil of the world brought to him by the devil and his demonic angels. Jesus survives this agony through his own spiritual power (the Father remains quite silent as far as one can tell). Then comes the pain and humiliation of the crucifixion. The only 'word' from the cross reported in Matthew's and Mark's gospels is the first verse of Psalm 22, 'My God, my God, why have you forsaken me?' (Mark 15.34). I feel that Jesus was doing something more than merely quoting a psalm, since the agonized call reported in the gospel is both damaging to the Christian witness and shows the terrible suffering of Jesus. Could he have lost faith in his call from God at this terminal stage of his life? To many believers this suggestion is as incredible as it is blasphemous, but we must remember that Jesus was entirely like us in his testing, but without sinning (putting himself first to the harm of other people) (Hebrews 4.15). It is not impossible that Jesus was suddenly assailed with severe doubts about either the validity of his mission or his success in carrying it out – or both together. Certainly his Father was eloquently silent during his Son's agony.

As in the early temptations in the wilderness, when the devil tempts Jesus to throw himself from the parapet of the temple (Matthew 4.5–7) but Jesus refuses to put his Father to the test, so now once more he is tempted to throw himself down from the cross (Matthew 27.39–40), but this time it was not merely a gesture to prove his great spiritual power but simply an act to preserve his life. The great proof of God's caring for him and what he stood for is completely absent, and the terrible cry from the cross may be interpreted in the light of this failure of supernatural help. Nevertheless Jesus held on to his life right until death closed this lamentable scene; he showed what it meant to be of human stock, and the soldiers at the foot of the cross were the first to express their admiration. He did not lose his nerve when death alone awaited him. From this we can derive a greater definition of faith than that which we considered in Chapter 7. Faith is continuing on one's way when all apparent hope has been removed. It was the final way of the cross, and it is pursued, albeit unknowing of its full consequences, when we too move inexorably towards dissolution at some time in our lives.

The difference between Jesus' agony and ours lies in the magnitude of his mission and service and the consequent sorrow at the final denouement. By contrast we are, to quote Psalm 90.5–6, mortals whom God cuts off, and are asleep in death. We are like grass that sprouts; though in the morning it flourishes and shoots up, by evening it droops and withers. In Chapter 1 I strongly praised those people who are incurably afflicted with diseases or handicaps that severely curtail the quality of their lives, but nevertheless soldier on in a faith that goes far beyond rational hope – the blind, the deaf, the paraplegics and those who suffer from other types of severe crippling, epileptics and diabetics under poor control because of the nature of their illness, and above all those who struggle courageously with mental disease. Few of these people arouse long-lasting sympathy, especially epileptics and the mentally ill, and so they are obliged to go on in spite of the darkness that so often accompanies their travail. All too often nobody wants to know, any more than they did the passion of Christ, and yet in each case a hope of supernatural quality keeps them on the path of life, just as it did Jesus, until the mercy of God decrees a time of generous withdrawal to the state that is to inform us all once the body has gone.

Desolation courageously confronted is usually succeeded by consolation as a new approach to reality is shown us. And so we can make use of our present sadness to move timidly and yet with purpose into what life holds in store for us. To make the most of an unfortunate event or a personal tragedy is the way of life shown by an emotionally mature person; there is little railing at God, or providence, but rather a determined effort to flow into the new situation, unpleasant though it may be, and see how much it can be used for further experimentation in the way of constructive living. This is the intelligent, emotionally mature human response to misfortune of any kind. When such a circumstance happens to me I always thank God first that the damage has been no worse than it is, then I pick myself up and note the extent of the misfortune and determine what can be done about it. I assume that my negligence has been the root cause of the trouble, and make a note of this for further reference. It is better to concentrate on one's own attitude than start by blaming other people, unless of course there has been an accident involving more than one person, when all the workings of the legal process may have to be involved. Consolation implies hope, as in the matters I have just discussed. The consolation comes primarily from the Holy Spirit giving us a completely new strength to face our future life, whether it be a bereavement or an injustice that evades the legal process. 'If in some province you witness the oppression of the poor and the denial of right and justice, do not be surprised at what goes on, for every official has a mightier one set over him, and the highest keeps watch over them all. The best thing for a country is a king whose own lands are well tilled' (Ecclesiastes 5.8–9).

But what hope did the earthly Jesus have in front of him? He died nobly, but the forces of injustice had scored a great victory. The same consideration applies to the victims of injustice who have been killed in every generation. In these instances desolation had proceeded to a silence that was not at all communicative, but was simply an indication that all living processes had come to an end. On a much less harrowing note this can be said of all of us who make the great transition which we call death. The death of Jesus seen from the point of view of Good Friday is not only the tragic failure of a noble mission but also the triumph of injustice and cruelty over all the finer qualities of human nature. The subsequent resurrection event gives an answer to this hard question. When Jesus arose again on the third day, a new man had come with the amazing re-appearance. He was no longer subject to the limitations of the physical body, but could come and go where he pleased. The tragedy of the passion was succeeded by the spontaneous joy of giving new life to the very weak and cowardly disciples who not long before had retreated from their Master. He had changed, and was now capable of changing his disciples in a way that was only begun while he was in the world with them. The existential proof of Jesus' resurrection, that clearly transcends any purely rational explanation such as we often hear at present, was the very real resurrection of the disciples from nearly dead individuals to vibrantly alive friends who were soon to spread the knowledge of their Master throughout the length and breadth of the Roman Empire. In Christ therefore, desolation had proceeded to transformation, the emergence of a new person who still, two millennia later, remains the pattern of a fully realized human being, a constant challenge to those of us with faint hearts and agnostic intellects.

Can one say the same, if to a much lesser degree, of the innocent prison-camp victims whose witness has so disgraced the twentieth century? And what about the young who have been stricken by fatal diseases like cancer, or whose lives have been terminated by terrible accidents? Here an eye of faith is needed; not the fundamentalistic faith contained in a holy book or a religious tradition, nor exactly the heroic faith we have been describing above which persists when all reasonable hope has been renounced. It is a fundamental faith in the nature of the human even when their kind have been responsible for monstrous crimes and tortures. The glory of human creativity in the form of great music, art and literature, to say nothing of scientific research devoted to the service of the entire created order, gives us a view to what we all might aspire, within the limitations of our own gifts and talents, when we move beyond the demands and expectations of the little ego and embrace the whole of life in self-giving devotion. Value judgements are the heart of the matter: faith can be defined as the capacity to choose the nobler of two propositions and to work towards its fulfilment. Nobility in this respect involves the three ultimate values: beauty, truth and goodness (better defined as love, inasmuch as the aim of love is to help each person to be themselves as God would have them be). There is clearly a close link between faith in the ultimate goodness of the human despite all evidence to the contrary, and a faith that persists when all apparent hope has been destroyed.

A great deal depends on the environment around those about to make the great transition of death, whether in a concentration camp or a hospital. Those serving in hospices for the dying know the matter very well; they flow out in pure love to their patients, so that nothing is too good for them. They are treated, perhaps for the first time, as people who matter in a world that is shortly to lose them to the unknown realm of death, that 'undiscover'd country from whose bourn no traveller returns', to quote from Hamlet's famous soliloquy. Once an individual's self-esteem can be affirmed, a new person may break through and greet the great mystery of the afterlife with considerable conviction, especially when they are met by figures of people whom they knew earlier on in their life. In the end we grasp the full meaning of the life

97

beyond death by personal experience in the depth of the soul. In other words, when we are quite still, the knowledge of immortality is not far from us. The evidences of survival of death culled from parapsychological sources are of most use to those who are investigating the subject; those who are making the move dynamically have a more personal experience once the overlying fear has dissipated in a friendly atmosphere.

We will know the change from the earthly clod we so often show ourselves to the diaphanous being that is our deeper nature once we are freed from dependence on worldly things, not so bad in themselves but imprisoning when our whole life is dedicated to them. I feel that the type of person who has died in the hell of a concentration camp will likewise know much more about themselves in the new life they are about to enter. If they have been able to comport themselves with nobility to their fellow prisoners while in one of these dark places of hell, they will step onwards to the place of light and love where much new information will be given them. In the end values do count, and if we can master the discipline of living responsibly even when we are surrounded by disorder and cruelty, we will not be the losers in what is to reveal itself once our passions are spent, and we can rest with thoughtful hope on to the future before us. This is the faith that gives substance to our hopes, no matter how muted they may be in a moment of crisis, and convinces us of realities we do not see.

Great masters of prayer tell us with one accord that we cannot reach the full practice of prayer until we have spent our time in the desert, rather like Jesus before the three temptations in the wilderness, and more especially the final temptation to despair at the time of his death. One can only pray effectively when the ego is moved consciously out of the way, and the deeper soul allowed to relay the love of God to the whole personality, and from that personality to the entire world in the work of intercession. Until we have traversed the valley of desolation we will see ourselves as the master of the world; assuredly not the whole world itself, for I speak here of our inner universe which we feel we know tolerably well. That it is in intimate connection with the worlds of other people will be something hardly available to its understanding, and so any real communication between it and the greater world will be impossible. The desert experience of desolation breaks down many mental barriers, and at last the previously invisible world is accessible to the individual through the mediation of an enlightened soul. It is then that silence ceases to be a dead, or even an embarrassing experience, but becomes a truly communicative one.

When we are truly ourselves in the fresh wind of desolation, we can start to live like responsible people, no longer attached to the opinions and prejudices of our fellows but true to our own nature. At that point we can enter a collegial relationship with many more of our like-minded associates. This is indeed the way for real friendships to commence and flourish.

It should finally be noted that desolation is not the same as depression. The former is a very tragic mood, the latter a disease when it assumes clinical proportions, with its disastrous lack of self-esteem, change in sleep rhythm, feeling of utter hopelessness and tendency to precipitate suicide. Desolation is not often devoid of underlying hope even in a desperate situation. However, a situation of desolation may trigger off depression in an individual already predisposed to the condition.

Two Shakespeare sonnets have been of great value to me in periods of desolation.

Poor soul, the centre of my sinful earth –
My sinful earth, these rebel powers array –
Why dost thou pine within and suffer dearth,
Painting thy outward walls so costly gay?
Why so large cost, having so short a lease,
Dost thou upon thy fading mansion spend?
Shall worms, inheritors of this excess,
Eat up thy charge? Is this thy body's end?
Then, soul, live thou upon thy servant's loss,
And let that pine to aggravate thy store;
Buy terms divine in selling hours of dross;
Within be fed, without be rich no more;
  So shalt thou feed on Death, that feeds on men;
  And Death once dead, there's no more dying then.

When, in disgrace with Fortune and men's eyes,
I all alone beweep my outcast state,
And trouble deaf heaven with my bootless cries,
And look upon myself, and curse my fate,
Wishing me like to one more rich in hope,
Featured like him, like him with friends possest,
Desiring this man's art and that man's scope,
With what I most enjoy contented least;
Yet in these thoughts myself almost despising –
Haply I think on thee: and then my state,
Like to the Lark at break of day arising
From sullen earth, sings hymns at Heaven's gate;
   For thy sweet love rememb'red such wealth brings
   That then I scorn to change my state with Kings.

I also like Emily Dickinson's inspiration.

To learn the transport by the pain
As blind men learn the sun,
To die of thirst suspecting
That brooks in meadows run,

To stay the homesick, homesick feet
Upon a foreign shore,
Haunted by native land the while,
And blue beloved air –

This is the sovereign anguish,
This is the signal woe.
These are the patient laureates
Whose voices trained below,

Ascend in ceaseless carol,
Inaudible indeed
To us the duller scholars
Of the mysterious bard.

One is reminded of Paul Tillich's words, 'The faith which makes
the courage of despair possible is the acceptance of the power of
being, even in the grip of non-being'. Tillich calls this 'the
courage to be', the title of possibly his best-known book (*The
Courage to Be* (New Haven and London: Yale University Press,
1962), p. 176). Simone Weil says, 'Only if man passes through

terror and anguish can he retain his will to love' (what is at stake is clinging to God's love, despite all the darkness and absence of God). Dietrich Bonhoeffer at the end of his *Letters and Papers from Prison* comes to very much the same conclusion when he speaks challengingly but confusingly about the death of God. Karl Rahner is clearer when he says, 'He who does not love mystery does not know God, for he does not see the true and only God'. Martin Luther speaks of 'the faith which has learnt to stand on nothingness'. (These quotations come from Elisabeth Ott's book *Die dunkle Nacht der Seele – Depression* (Schaffhausen: Novalis Verlag, 1982).) In our travail and feeling of guilt we may take comfort from 1 John 3.19–20, 'This is how we shall know that we belong to the realm of truth, and reassure ourselves in his sight where conscience condemns us; for God is greater than our conscience and knows all'.

It is indeed a privilege to be human and experience these deep emotions that bring us to the very core of our being, the soul where the indomitable spirit burns with a divine fire that will never be extinguished. In the end it will take its place humbly yet majestically in the uncreated light of God, of which it is a mere terrestrial outpost in our world of space and time. But through the divine guidance informing us by way of that spirit we can never be content until we know the truth. This truth is no exotic, esoteric theory or instruction confined to a favoured group who have scoured the very universe for knowledge, for ultimate gnosis into the secrets of the divine. It bursts forth in self-giving love to the very weakest of our fellow creatures. In that moment of sacrifice our eyes are opened so that we are able to see clearly for the first time in our lives. It is thus that desolation may pass through a phase of consolation to an experience of inspiration, in which truths of even greater magnitude are revealed to us as we pass onward in the strange, savage, beautiful journey of life.

10 Forgiveness

The spirit of forgiveness pours out like a precious balm on a wounded soul. To be forgiven is the first step, and this requires first a candid admission that we were wrong in our attitudes and behaved wrongly in consequence. The soul expands in the warmth of a relief that, although it was culpable, it is nevertheless embraced in a love that will never depart from it. Love, as we discussed in Chapter 7, is a way of willed response which desires the persons to be themselves as God would have them be, and acts accordingly. The action is firstly pure silent prayer, in the course of which the inspiration of the Holy Spirit touches the depths and guides one into the proper way of action. The action that follows is no more one's personal response with its inevitably selfish component no matter how detached one feels, but rather the Spirit of God working through a cleansed individual, a true instrument of grace and peace, whose labours bring reassurance and calm delight to the one to whom service is expended. Forgiveness comes from God not the human; in the words of Alexander Pope's cliché, 'To err is human, to forgive divine'.

On the surface this seems a rather extreme view until we examine ourselves and our motives in detached clarity. Forgiveness in its real, embracing sense is not something that we can produce at a pinch, it is not an attitude that we can forthwith assume by a simple act of will, for we cannot come down to the position of the sinner, the one who has erred against us. We will inevitably approach him or her from a summit of rectitude, bestowing our pardon on them, but not really relating as person to person. What we are actually doing is pardoning the other individual, who in turn may be mightily relieved inasmuch as any impending punishment has passed mercifully from them like a menacing cloud in a pleasant, coolly blue summer sky with its threat of a shower just when we were organizing some outdoor activity. But there is no real relationship with the offender any more than there would have been in a court of law: the magistrate may be especially considerate, but the legal distance between him or her and the defendant makes any really human contact well nigh impossible.

I pardon from a situation of advantage, whether social, legal or moral; I forgive as person to person. My own heart is strangely warmed by an affection that has an interesting element of relief in it. As I am open to forgiving my fellow human, so the forgiveness that flows through my soul and informs my intellect with its bodily response assures me inwardly that I too have been forgiven. One begins to see how much unpleasant emotional debris resides in oneself, and the act of God's pure love cleanses one of much resentment, and not a little sinfulness also, as the love radiates to the person due to be forgiven. No wonder the relevant clause in the Lord's Prayer speaks of God forgiving us our sins as we forgive those who sin against us. If we are to be forgiven it is not sufficient to confess our sins to God and ask for forgiveness; we have also to open ourselves to the masked resentment we entertain against others and ask that this too may be expunged. True forgiveness has a transforming effect on the character both of the sinner and the one sinned against.

As long as we hold doggedly on to past associations, we close ourselves to God's renewing love. We remain *in statu quo*, and our responses have something of a perpetual gramophone record about them. But once we can let go of the past in faith, a new spiritual consciousness will infuse our being; where there was a frigid inactivity there is now a warm flowing out to the moment at hand. If I pardon you I may well not completely trust you; I shall be careful not to put you into any position wherein you may injure or betray me in the future. On the other hand, my forgiveness starts a new relationship between us; bygones are really bygones, and I start from a fresh beginning. Can the same be true of a criminal who has paid the price of their crime and misdemeanour? This is a very hard question, inasmuch as it might be wrong to tempt a frail brother with the world's goods, especially in the face of poverty such as most of the world's population have to confront. In a situation like this it seems that common sense should prevail in respect of the weakness of the offending party, but one should always remember one's own frailties and flow out to our weaker friend in love. A very disordered personality may fling our concern in our faces, and here the assistance of professional carers is well nigh essential for the well-being of us both. If truth is evaded, one moves from love to sentimentality, and considerable harm may accrue not only to us but to society as a whole. St Paul writes, 'We are to maintain the truth in a spirit of love; so shall we fully grow up into Christ' (Ephesians 4.15).

This rather agonized discussion shows us that forgiveness comes from God but it is to be tempered by the human according to experience and wisdom. The circumstances determine our reaction, and we should not be influenced by a feeling of guilt because we cannot do more than our share at any one time. But the really important matter is harbouring an attitude of forgiveness even when we are dealing with incorrigible people. What we may not be able to effect directly can still be set in action by the power of prayer. Such prayer does not attempt to enlist God's intervention – he surely is aware of the fundamental problem more than we can ever hope to be – but to transmit God's love to the person for whom we intercede. A great deal depends on how receptive he or she is as to the possibility of a response, as well as its nature and magnitude; these are aspects of prayer that do not lie in our control. If forgiveness is to have a real effect, the one who has caused the trouble should emit humility and gratitude; if this response is forthcoming we both can start from a fresh footing and work towards becoming firm friends.

The two emotions that spark off forgiveness are guilt, which we have already considered, and anger. This is classified as one of the seven deadly sins, the others being pride, covetousness, lust, gluttony, envy and sloth. In everyday life anger requires a more profound analysis than merely to be called a sin; it may be less categorically condemned, for it is a spontaneous response to injustice whether this be real or merely imaginary. Anger can be regarded as a natural defence against destructive people who would otherwise trample over us. Such an anti-social attitude may be quite deliberate or blandly unwitting, but the effect is similar. There is therefore a legitimate place for anger in our psychological make-up, but it must be released with circumspection; above all it must never take control, otherwise the personality rapidly becomes isolated in a darkness which excludes any reflection other than the cause of the anger. This soon becomes a focus of destruction that affords us great satisfaction, comparable with sexual stimulation and sometimes providing it quite unobtrusively. Meanwhile the other, and far more important, problems of life are hidden beneath the acrid fumes of smouldering anger. Indeed, when anger takes over our life's concern, it rapidly obliterates all our finer feelings, in this way diverting our attention from the essential work of service with its attendant growth of the personality, so that we become prisoners in a static self-absorption that alienates us progressively from the lives of our friends and colleagues.

In this way anger which commences as a natural response to injustice can rapidly assert a pernicious control over us that seeks to eliminate anything that blocks its way. We are charting the rapid unfolding of anger to hatred; it is a characteristic of those political and religious movements that refuse to tolerate any dissident voices in their midst. These are easily magnified as enemies of society by angry fanatics. The witness of history bears a bitter record of such hatred finding its outlet in actions of terrifying destructiveness like the genocidal atrocities of our century. There is always a cause for anger, whether personal, communal or national, however childish and ill-informed it may appear to detached outsiders. As we read in Proverbs 14.10, 'The heart knows its own bitterness, and in its joy a stranger has no part'. When one investigates the cause of the bitterness that overflows in passionate anger, one is well advised to suspend judgement and rather enter into the inner life of the individual or the group. The gift of empathy, being able to project our personality into that of the person or group we are attempting to comprehend, is very valuable in such an undertaking. The basic emotion that precipitates anger is often fear, which in turn shows itself in a belief that injustice, even to a criminal extent, is being practised upon us. Some fear is clearly justified, but often it is quite plainly baseless and morbid, coming into the psychiatric category of paranoia, a state of mental ill-health in which the victim has delusions of being persecuted. A delusion is a false belief that is held despite all contrary evidence, and when it is extended into a system of ideas that influences the entire way of life, it not only excludes the person progressively from the company of their fellows but can also lead to violent exchanges as their anger mounts and can find no relief in normal social intercourse.

When such fears and delusions affect only one person, their error is obvious enough to the outsider, and the appropriate action may be taken, but when an entire community is similarly afflicted the national and international consequences may be of cataclysmic extent. In this way a vanquished nation may refuse to accept its defeat and adapt itself to the new situation in which it finds itself. Instead of this it is liable to look for scapegoats who can be blamed for the defeat, and even worse, for snatching the food from the remainder of the community. The scapegoat may differ in religious tradition from the majority of the people, practise a less acceptable life-style or be of demonstrably different ethnic origin from the native inhabitants of the country. Such 'deviants' are frequently more prosperous than many of their indigenous neighbours, in which case it is easy enough for the national paranoia to attribute exclusive practices to the materially successful ones in the midst of the honest community, succeeding, as it were, by defrauding the others. As anyone with historical knowledge can see, all this happened to Germany during the Nazi regime; if only Germany had been treated more magnanimously at the Treaty of Versailles at the end of the First World War, the terrible sequence of national events that ended with Hitler and all that came from him might have been averted. The lesson was far better learned at the end of the Second World War, when Germany was treated much more kindly. Now we know that war has no victors, though it may still have to be waged against a country that starts hostilities in order to gain territorial advantage at the expense of its neighbours.

This diversion into the realms of recent history as well as the consideration of a more private, personal type of anger shows us how important it is that feelings of anger should be acknowledged at once, and the cause of that anger dealt with expeditiously. Apart from anger flaring up into a mighty conflagration of lethal hatred, it may also be dangerously repressed and eat cancerously into the soul. In such a case there is an initial injustice that has to be borne with an attitude of hopeless resignation. This is the typical response of people who are weak and are obliged to accept physical or mental abuse, and tolerate it indefinitely. If they were temerarious enough to resist and fight back, they could be severely manhandled and sustain serious injuries. The unfortunate child who is subjected to abuse, usually physically and sometimes sexually, is a typical example of the effects of this form of cruelty. The poor child's self-esteem is flattened, and beneath this psychological mutilation there festers a veritable sea of anger that cannot be readily expressed. Instead of outward expression, the anger eats into the personality where it produces a feeling of impotence both in the management of the person's own life and in participation in the world's greater affairs. The despondency may deepen and broaden progressively into a mounting depression that may assume clinical proportions in the type of individual predisposed to really severe depression as contrasted with a persistent despondency that recovers once the cause of the trouble has been removed.

Unsatisfied ambitions lead to another deadly sin, envy and its close relative, jealousy. I prefer to understand envy as a state of mind in which one covets other people's possessions or personal qualities like beauty or intelligence. Jealousy seems to proceed further: the fortunate person is disliked on account of their gifts to the extent of wanting to diminish that individual up to the point of their total destruction. This is achieved not so much by an act of physical violence that might kill as by speech which first casts aspersions upon the moral character of the person, then their skills and talents are subtly denigrated until in the end they are reduced to the level of sheer nonentity, which is, of course, the exact replica of the aggrieved party. Slander claims many more victims than does physical violence. The pen and its articulating organ, the tongue, are indeed mightier than the sword, as Edward George Bulwer-Lytton wrote in his poem 'Richelieu', except that he did not include the tongue in his celebrated observation. His omission is made good in James 3.6–10, which begins, 'The tongue is like a fire, representing in our body the whole wicked world. It pollutes our whole being, it sets the whole course of our existence alight, and its flames are fed by hell.' The writer also observes that no one can subdue the tongue, which is an evil thing, restless and charged with deadly venom. Fortunately the tongue can also speak kindly and with generosity, but only when the spirit of goodwill informs its action. This is not compatible with jealousy or anger.

When we consider the hatred of communities against deviant groups, there is usually an odour of jealousy that inflames the latent force of fear and incapacity. Whatever we especially denounce or deride not infrequently covers a weak spot in our own character; thus the seeker after social advancement may attack the upper classes and those who covet wealth not infrequently deride rich people. Snobbery does not lose its humour by being inverted by unconscious jealousy.

All these aberrations of character, hatred, jealousy, snobbery and covetousness, speak of an inner anger that has not been properly confronted let alone assuaged. When we have been denied the self-esteem which is the due of any sensitive person, we seek to attain it in various subterfuges which build up the ego structure on airy fantasies. When the fall comes, as it does without fail, the collapse of the person may be well nigh complete. It is evident that anger has to be confronted directly, without either approval or condemnation, and its source uncovered. Much anger follows the gross injustice of abuse when we were helpless children. In the same fashion various religious and ethnic groups have been subjected to virulent cruelty throughout the centuries, but in none more systematically than our own. Those who have perished can at least carry their secret with them to the after-life, however we may conceive this, but the survivors have a terrible burden of implicit or explicit injustice to carry.

While their contemporaries elsewhere are apparently living prosperous, fertile lives, they themselves are placed in the shadows of a broken personality, not infrequently accompanied by a ruined body also, the victim of cruel torture. One can hardly forget Job putting his case desperately before an ominously silent God, or the Psalmist not infrequently telling God to get moving in helping his chosen people. Some suffering is clearly well deserved, but much pain comes to people who have not been conspicuously remiss in their social and religious duties.

There are two thoughts that may extend our anguish about the unmerited suffering visited on luckless individuals or ethnic groups: firstly there is a belief in retribution and healing visited on the personality in the life beyond death. I personally accept the premise underlying this comforting reflection, but I cannot still my conscience with its outraged sense of decency by ruminating on a hypothesis that will not face the immediate inadequacy of the world's present state. It is far too easy a 'cop out', a means of evading present disorder with visions of pie (or decayed meat for the evil doers in society) in the sky. Religion that stresses a working out of present distress in terms of rewards and punishments in our posthumous existence does not ring completely true, inasmuch as those retributions are contingent on the life we have led in this world. The occasional saint will have transcended all the grievances of the present in a vision of God that is of eternal quality, but most of us lesser beings will take our misery with us, a misery that prevents proper fellowship with those around us in any society, whether mundane or on the other side of physical death.

The other thought that may extend our anguish about the unmerited suffering visited upon unfortunate people is the deeper reflection that we are all parts of the one body of humanity, indeed of creation. We cannot expect to remain untouched even if our own lives have been of exemplary virtue. The same thought applies to the suffering and pain of little children and infants who fall victim to lethal diseases and die either rapidly or else after a period of painful encounter with the forces of darkness that so frequently seem to govern our little world. It has been my painful duty to attend the families of a number of such small children who have succumbed to cancers of the brain. In each case I have been humbled by the advanced state of understanding shown by the little ones, who know quite clearly what is in store for them in this life, and are more concerned about their parents' grief than their own condition. They seem to possess a preternatural sense of their future in the eternity of life, and seek to give some guidance to those who are mourning around them. Little people like these – and their simple adult representatives by extension – not only chasten my own self-centredness but also give me immense respect for the human race, and seem to illuminate the way ahead for us all once we begin to lose self-consciousness with all its obstacles. It was the same selfish ignorance that interfered with Peter's being able to accept the full nature of Christ's impending sacrifice after he had confessed that Jesus was the Messiah, the Son of the living God (the sequence of Matthew 16.13–23 describes the full episode, Peter as usual clouding his spark of cosmic vision by thoughts of his own vulnerability, which he projects on to his Master). St Paul puts the matter in a somewhat comparable light when he writes in Colossians 1.24, 'It is now my joy to suffer for you; for the sake of Christ's body, the church, I am completing what still remains for Christ to suffer in my own person'.

No cruelty committed in this world is without its future repercussions. To be sure, the perpetrators have the primary price to pay, but society itself dare not wash its hands of the matter and claim virtuous exemption from the fruits of individual misdemeanour. It too was involved in the education and welfare of the miscreant, who was in all probability badly treated in their childhood and youth. The tendency for child abusers to have been similarly treated when they were young is very well recognized; this does not exonerate the present crime, but it does show us all how careful we have to be in our attitudes to other people. As Jesus would say to us, 'Do not judge, and you will not be judged. For as you judge others, so you will yourselves be judged, and whatever measure you deal out to others will be dealt to you' (Matthew 7.1–2). It is my belief that the world's saints help to lift up the world from the slough of despair that seems to enclose us all when we read of the many cruelties that humans are so adept at visiting on their fellow kind and on creation as a whole. These saints include the nameless ones also who live decent lives and serve the community by their example of patience and courage in the face of destructive disease, no less than those who live more actively in the world and may sacrifice their lives for their fellows in circumstances of destruction and terror.

Such suffering brings us all to a higher regard for our sacred calling to be God's priests, and I believe can produce a real change in the character of the person as well as an inspiration of their mind to a nobler way of living. The mind tends to play down the inspiration in the course of time whereas a real change in the character persists. The conversion of Saul of Tarsus on the road to Damascus is a case in point: the Jewish persecutor of the early Christians became the great St Paul, the apostle to the Gentiles primarily within the great Roman Empire but subsequently throughout the world as a result of his letters. His sufferings for the church, well documented in his letters to the Corinthians, have been the prototype of the sufferings of humanity as a whole for the better life in Christ, which, when properly practised, will change the whole face of humanity. We still await that day, but only when we all have come through the sufferings of body and mind, will we be able to play our part in the completion of a transformed world.

The burning question remains: how is the unjustly injured person to deal with their resentment, their burning anger, their flaming hatred? As I have already said, it is far better for these destructive emotions to be brought to the surface than lie buried deep in the psyche where they fester and lead to a crippling depression. The answer, of course, is by the practice of forgiveness, but this is not so easily effected. The situation bears some resemblance to bereavement with its emotional concomitant of grieving for the beloved. After an immediate period of shock there follows a prolonged emotional trough of sorrow, anger, guilt and shame, all of which have to be worked through without evading their harrowing inner desolation or their possibly embarrassing communal manifestations of tears and bitterness. It may take up to two years for a normal emotional life to be resumed. (A dead child is never replaced in its mother's or father's thoughts, but the parents have to proceed with the demands of common life, since time does not stand still to fit in with our moods of desolation.)

The same approach is useful in communicating with people who are consumed with anger and hatred. There is a time for the outer display to be faced with complete acceptance. Meanwhile time passes by, the memories of those supporting the person become increasingly dulled as they of necessity resume their own lives, and they rather impatiently expect the victim to follow in the same direction, as indeed the wise and self-controlled do. 'For mortals depart to their everlasting home, and the mourners go about the street' (Ecclesiastes 12.5). Soon the mourners are obliged to return to their own private lives and businesses, but whereas the one who has died proceeds to the life beyond death, those they have left behind will have to play the game of life with their friends and colleagues, otherwise they will find themselves left behind with few to care about them. In respect of getting back on to one's own feet we can do no better than consider the positive life-affirmation characteristic of the Jews. One of the most inspiring features of their painful history of persecution and attempted destruction has been their capacity to come up to the surface and resume their interesting, rewarding and highly constructive lives despite continuing anti-Semitic prejudice. Their unique contribution to the affairs of the mind and the spirit has remained undulled despite even the radical attempt at their total annihilation practised by the Nazis in our own century.

This does not imply that a terrible racial memory of injustice and cruelty can be simply erased. It remains ineradicably fixed to warn the people to take good care in the future, but meanwhile their precious life has to be preserved and enjoyed while their faculties are in good order. There are some of us who find it almost impossible to let go of the past, letting bygones be bygones; they live in a constant atmosphere of grief and hatred, with desires for revenge lurking not too far in the background of their thoughts. It seems that little can be done to expunge their memories other than by the grace of God; even this cannot effect a foothold until the person's will is motivated towards a change in perspective with a deep desire to start a new life. The way in which we can be of most use is by listening in quiet sympathy to their repeated accounts of past events and assimilating the bitterness that pours out from them. A communicative silence is of vital importance, not the dead silence of helplessness but the living silence of deep participation, during which the Holy Spirit is liable to inspire us with conciliatory words. Patience may become strained, because many such people revel in their grievances, positively enjoying being miserable. These are beyond human help until the Holy Spirit works through their damaged minds. Sometimes a change in attitude may follow a serious accident or illness, in the course of which the individual is obliged to face a critical situation of life and death as immediate as that of the concentration camps of long ago. Once the overriding value of simply being alive has been recognized, however fleetingly, there is a small opening for kindness and concern to enter the hard shell, the carapace, of the soul.

The alternative response to injustice and cruelty is a mounting depression. It is here that psychotherapy can be of great value in disclosing the source of the trouble, which is often related to abuse during childhood. It is not without significance that a number of distinguished Jewish victims of the Holocaust who survived and seemed to have come to terms with the terrible events, suddenly committed suicide many years after the end of the Second World War. It could well be that they simply could not tolerate or cope with the memories of the past when these came flooding relentlessly into consciousness once more. There has been a notorious tendency of late for some people to deny, or at least to play down, the enormity of the Nazi death camps. While the main factor in this denial has undoubtedly been neo-Nazism, or fascism, among the determined promulgators of this unhistorical view, there has possibly been another factor at work as well: the difficulty that uncommitted people may have in accepting, let alone assimilating, the evil in question. What is morally repugnant can easily be ignored while we lead comfortable suburban lives replete with the good things that encompass us. It is questioned nowadays whether it would indeed be a

sensible thing to dwell less conscientiously on the Holocaust and
to move on to more constructive contemporary matters.

I believe that history plays a vital part in showing us the way in
which the human psyche works over the many centuries of
recorded events. We turn our backs on history to our own grave
disadvantage. But the horrors of the past, of which the fascist
concentration camps are merely items, albeit terrifying ones, in a
long pageant stretching from the earliest records until our tragic
century, are not to be forgotten. They also illustrate the nobility
of individual sacrifice amid the carnage of the multitudes. On the
other hand, it is unwise to dwell on these matters. They simply
arouse hatred and a desire for revenge when they are concentrated upon to the virtual exclusion of the concurrent world
situation. If any of us were to reflect on the sins that were
committed against us during our life up to the present time, we
might lose ourselves in bitterness and schemes of vengeance.
Fortunately if we have a spiritual background, one in which God
is the central presence of our lives, our attention is soon directed
inwards to the less acceptable elements of our own character, and
then we begin to seek forgiveness even more than justice for our
own claims.

Terrible cruelty like that visited upon the victims of concentration camps and similar places of torture is not subject to
human forgiveness except in the wake of a great downpouring of
divine love that transforms our ego-centred personality to a soul-
directed creature full of love and compassion. St Paul writes,
' "Vengeance is mine," says the Lord, "I will repay" ' (Romans
12.19, quoting Deuteronomy 32.35). Even this great truth can be
a snare if we wait impatiently for God's justice to be visited on
the objects of our own wrath. We have to learn to let go of the
past, of the present too, and indeed of everything that appertains
to us personally. It is a matter of considering the dictum we have
already noticed: 'Whoever wants to save his life will lose it, but
whoever loses his life for my sake and for the gospel's will save it'
(Mark 8.35). If one looks down upon cruelty and suffering from
a purely personal point of view, the one advantage that strikes
one is the gift of discrimination, of being able to disentangle the
ego life that is due for destruction no matter how well it is

crammed with good things, and the soul life that triumphs over all adversity to know the kingdom of God in its very midst but usually obscured by misconceptions that masquerade as the truth. It is sad that the unthinking practice of religion can easily degenerate into one of these misconceptions.

William Blake's poem, 'A Poison Tree', one of the *Songs of Experience*, shows how the repression of anger can breed malevolence. It is written as a sharp warning.

I was angry with my friend:
I told my wrath, my wrath did end.
I was angry with my foe:
I told it not, my wrath did grow.

And I watered it in fears,
Night and morning with my tears:
And I sunned it with smiles,
And with soft deceitful wiles.

And it grew both day and night,
Till it bore an apple bright.
And my foe beheld it shine,
And he knew that it was mine.

And into my garden stole,
When the night had veiled the pole;
In the morning glad I see,
My foe outstretched beneath the tree.

It is evident that forgiveness stands in a direct relationship with love: both come from God, and both bring us closer to him and to our fellows. Forgiveness precedes love in a situation of anger and resentment. We know that we have really forgiven the other person or the injustice of the past when we feel an inner expansion of the soul. The really unpleasant aspect of anger and resentment is the closed effect they have on us; they imprison us in an attitude of defensiveness and suspicion that will not let us be really free to communicate with other people. These must first be on our side before we can relate fully to them. Of course our friends should be both with us and beyond us in their own concerns and aspirations. If we demand absolute loyalty from them we limit their own relationships with other people, including those with whom we are in enmity. But once the spirit of forgiveness touches our soul, we can let go of the past, not ceasing to remember it but, far more important, ceasing to care overmuch about it. At last we can begin to live full lives, imbibing the waters of renewal and inspiring the air of freedom. This inner expansion is one of the greatest experiences of God's grace that we may know, and our hearts sing a jubilant song of gratitude. Joy reigns supreme in little jets of humour and love that cannot be suppressed. And what we send out is returned to us in full measure by all those around us, themselves wondering why they feel so happy and contented. The reason is that in the presence of God's love all their perennial worries and fears are taken up into God's presence, where they are resurrected to the light rather like the resurrection of Jesus' own disfigured body after the trial of its crucifixion.

When we are forgiven our own sins, we know of the relief and joy as a new life opens for us, and we enter the company of our peers as if nothing adverse had happened. Our gratitude is beyond description. When we in turn experience a sense of forgiveness for all the suffering we have been obliged to undergo, the new life rejoices in paeans of praise to God, the supreme Creator always making the old order new. In this way we have no doubt either that we are forgiven for our past sins or that we have completely forgiven the past for the injustice we have been obliged to bear. The two are closer together than would be apparent at first sight, for God forgives us when we sincerely want to forgive the other person. The clause in the Lord's Prayer referred to earlier on in the chapter is thus fulfilled, except that our forgiveness extends beyond personal matters to the world situation at large. The anger that we justly register in the face of cruelty is assuaged in a larger vision of wholeness of which forgiveness is the portal of entry.

We may end with some celebrated words of William Blake from his 'Auguries of Innocence':

A Robin Redbreast in a cage
Puts all Heaven in a rage . . .
A dog starv'd at his master's gate

Predicts the ruin of the State,
A horse misus'd upon the road
Calls to Heaven for human blood.
Each outcry of the hunted hare
A fibre from the brain doth tear,
A skylark wounded in the wing,
A cherubim does cease to sing . . .
The bat that flits at close of eve
Has left the brain that won't believe.

And so the indictment of human cruelty to the defenceless animal kingdom proceeds. Blake would be pleased that his protests against unkindness to animals are now taken so seriously that cruelty to them is currently a penal offence in many of the developed countries. Here is a good example of strong, poetic anger leading the way to a more civilized attitude to animal welfare. But if the concern goes out of hand, destructive 'animal rights' groups develop and flourish, which, apart from antagonizing society as a whole, strive to forbid the use of animals for experimental purposes. The loss to scientific research could be profound were these valuable procedures to be abandoned. On the other hand, meticulous care needs to be used in determining how far any procedure may be used. In a spirit of goodwill real advances can be made, which would be impossible in an atmosphere of prejudice and animosity. One longs for the day when all animal research will be unnecessary, but at present we have to be guided by what is expedient to our current needs.

All these sentiments, it could be argued, are admirable enough from the human point of view, albeit a trifle smug, but what about the animals? If their mental apparatus were advanced enough to retain memories such as we humans do, would they forgive us the suffering inflicted on their kind by the early vivisectors, who worked before general anaesthetics were known of or, in a later time, fully perfected in respect of putting the experimental animal out of all pain during the procedure? Living as we do in a pragmatic society, one which is not ashamed to see the end as justifying the means, most of us would regard the animals as necessary sacrifices for the advancement of scientific knowledge, whose aim is the relief of disease in both humans and animals. Those of a more cynical turn of mind would also see an ulterior aim: the publication of papers on scientific research as aiding the ambitions of young workers with an eye to professorships and international glory. Fortunately animal experimentation is much more closely monitored nowadays than in the past, a result of those groups who have the care of animals as their principal concern.

One hopes that, if those animals could understand what they were undergoing, they would give of themselves freely as sacrifices in humble imitation of Jesus Christ himself. This, I suppose, is how all human victims are best inspired in their own cruel pain as they move from this harsh world to what lies ahead for us all.

11 Awareness of mortality

When we are young our thoughts are directed forwards to the coming day; when we grow older our thoughts are often drawn involuntarily backwards to previous episodes in our life. If we are wise we do not resist this indrawing of consciousness, on the contrary we co-operate with its insight and start to reflect quietly yet deliberately on what we are shown. In my own life I was first taken back almost year by year to my boyhood and youth in South Africa, vignettes of which illuminate the early chapters of this book. Topography has always meant much to me, so that I could in my memory trace the very streets of Johannesburg, where I spent virtually all of my early life. The reminiscence brought back nostalgia and pain, as I came to my social ineptitude and paralysing shyness with renewed sensitivity. But the house in which I lived and received my domestic education remains a permanent landmark in my memory, rather sadly in fact, for when I revisited the suburb after I had been in England for about seven years, I could scarcely recognize either it or the locality. I returned to say farewell to my dying mother, and the house was in a state of disrepair even on the outside. It was in fact in the process of being sold at a ridiculously low price, for my father's state of mind caused him to dispense with it at any cost. Much of the city had also undergone radical alterations with the creation of motorways and the development of new areas of habitation. All this occurred in the late 1950s and when I came back once more some twenty years later to bid farewell to my aged father not too far off his own death, the place was scarcely the same as I knew it in my childhood.

There is nothing remarkable in all this, but what matters in my life is the memory I have retained as part of my life's journey, and I believe that memory is immortal: it will I am sure accompany me in the life I shall know after my physical body dies, as will the subsequent memories I have of my life in Britain in the various pursuits of postgraduate medical student, hospital doctor, pathologist, army medical officer, lecturer in pathology, investigator of paranormal healing, counsellor, church worker, and ultimately priest. The medical side ran concurrently with my priesthood until the lectureship came to its own end because of a failure of financial means in the institute that employed me, but within a year I was appointed priest-in-charge of the church in which I had previously acted as an assistant non-stipendiary. In the course of my 'spiritual' journey I was befriended and supported by a number of older people, nearly all women, and these have now not surprisingly died. Of greater poignancy is the death of some of my contemporaries, mostly in the medical field, but also some who accompanied me on the deeper journey of the soul, which is what the spiritual journey is about: the end is the vision of God. Some died fairly recently, but others a decade or more ago. I remember my South African contemporaries at school and university, and I have heard that some also are deceased. It happens that I have an especially acute memory, but in any case with the advance of years it is well recognized that distant childhood remembrance tends to persist, while one's memory for recent events becomes increasingly capricious. So far this embarrassing amnesia has not seriously afflicted me, but I have no doubt that the present spate of activities will also reach their end.

In the middle of the night I sometimes awaken, and find myself living momentarily in the past, one, two, three or even more decades ago, and the pain of realizing how old I now am (in my later sixties) is quite overwhelming. I have learned that there may be another factor involved in this temporary feeling of desolation, and this I shall discuss in Chapter 13. However, be this as it may, the death of old, partly forgotten contemporaries of long ago brings one up sharply to thoughts of one's own mortality and the fact of death. In waking consciousness I have an extremely positive view of death; I see it as a moment of great transition of consciousness from the limited perspective that the physical body necessarily imparts to the far greater freedom and vision of the soul at last broken free from its earthy moorings, and now able to participate in something of the felicity of an afterlife far closer to the vision of God. Indeed, I believe that during sleep I have a privileged work of accompanying some less experienced souls to the portal of the afterlife: they enter while I am turned back for further service on this side of the Styx. This duty of 'boatman' which seems peculiarly mine has been shown to me in a consciousness midway between sleep and waking, and has on occasions been corroborated by the unexpected death of someone who was close to me in a counselling situation. I knew that they were ill, even victims of inoperable cancer, but I had not anticipated their demise at that particular time and so suddenly. As a result, as I have already said, I have a very constructive view of the afterlife, and certainly not one that should fear death. All this shows that in any one mind there may be two contradictory attitudes, somehow managing to exist together in at least a superficial harmony. This is to be contrasted with wishful thinking on the one hand and frank hypocrisy on the other. Wishful thinking strives to evade the less acceptable aspects of reality by covering them with a fabric of oblivion; another metaphor would be that of sweeping them under the carpet of consciousness. Hypocrisy by contrast is well aware of the contradictory aspects of its assertions, but simply pretends to dismiss the less acceptable ones as non-existent. The hypocrite alternatively amuses and infuriates by their attitude of rectitude that is so clearly at variance with the life they lead. If we are wise we should start to see through these ways of faulty action by coming clean, at least to ourselves, about what is really happening deep within ourselves.

The conflict is between the conscious self and the vast tracts of the personal unconscious which merge with the considerably more spacious realm of the collective unconscious, in which our own experience of an inner level meets with that of the human mind in its collective experience. 'We belong to one another as parts of one body' (Ephesians 4.25). St Paul, if indeed he did actually write this letter, was referring to Christian believers, but twenty centuries have imparted a global consciousness to all humanity, indeed all creation, that makes our coinherence obvious to anyone with psychic sensitivity. In the early hours of the morning when we awaken from a deep sleep, the unconscious is much more at the surface than during active life at the height of daytime. We often tend to see matters in a peculiarly personal and biased light so that our worst suspicions are confirmed, and all our prejudices justified. Physiologically it may be that the brain is less well supplied with glucose at that time of comparative fasting; as in all such considerations it is wise to marry the physical and psychological rather than to separate them. Certainly the brain is immensely powerful in its sensitivity to changes in our internal environment, which in turn evoke emotional and other mental reactions. In this condition (in the early hours of the morning) we are more open to our true attitudes than in the heat of the day's work, when all that is adverse can be overlaid with exciting activities and positive thoughts. If we grow into our full humanity there is a corresponding marriage between the conscious and unconscious in our lives, so that finally nothing is, and need be, hid from our private inspection. This is the end of the psychoanalytic process, but not a few of us attain it by courage and the constant help of the Holy Spirit.

It is in this mature attitude, where faith joins ranks with reason and fear is sensibly illuminated by hope, that our response to death finds its most satisfying synthesis. Then nothing need be hidden from our awareness, and we may move ineluctably, yet peculiarly comfortingly, into the vast expanse of the unknown, which I suspect is closer to our knowledge than many daylight hours with their planned activities that so often follow a course that none of us would have predicted. It is therefore right to be terrified by the advent of death, the cessation of our mortal activities and our strange transition into the undiscovered country from whose bourn no traveller returns, to quote once more from Hamlet's famous soliloquy. Jesus' agony in the precincts of Gethsemane (Matthew 26.36–45) was due in part to his awareness of his imminent death, though I personally sense a far greater battle with the concerted forces of evil that had merely revealed their hand during the time when he was tempted in the wilderness at the beginning of his ministry (Matthew 4.1–11). But then I have no difficulty in accepting the presence of evil forces outside the human personality that can create havoc when one is spiritually unguarded. If this is so, it could be that all states of concerted terror have a demonic component working alongside our own unprotected psyche, and only too apt to create trouble if once given the opportunity. When we come more properly to ourselves in a wider consciousness, we can grapple with the darkness around us, while more positive forces of light sustain us in the great encounter now at our very doorstep. When believers confess their fear at the prospect of death, feeling that a really sincere faith would move beyond all doubt and terror, I assure them quite composedly that they need feel no shame. To be a Christian does not lift one above all mortal concerns into a world of spiritual beauty; on the contrary, such a confession of Christian faith brings one more solidly down to earth than ever before. The object of the work is to elevate the earth to be a place of spiritual beauty, in the course of which we all undergo at least something of the passion that Christ experienced fully in his own ministry. Of course Christ is with us in our mortal journey, and his Spirit infuses and inspires us for each day's work, but he leaves no path untraversed whereby we too may know something of his suffering. The end is our own participation in his glory, which first revealed itself at his resurrection. Therefore we have to become progressively acquainted with the totality of our own nature, the unbecoming no less than the admirable, the terrifying as well as the strengthening. The end of this rather unremitting process of self-disclosure is the emergence of a fully integrated person, 'the attainment of the unity inherent in our faith and in our knowledge of the Son of God – to mature manhood, measured by nothing less than the full stature of Christ' (Ephesians 4.12–13). To be sure this passage applies specifically to the infant Christian community, but it also reflects the essence of the hope in the life of the individual believer.

It is the physical body that fears death, and understandably too, for its purpose is the provision of a vehicle and a dwelling place for the soul on this side of the grave. While we are alive here, it is necessary that the body is well taken care of in order to provide a mechanism for the soul's outer action in the world. The healthier we are, the more efficient may be our work, and the more help we can be for all that lies around us. We soon learn to care considerately for our brethren no matter how outrageously they may have behaved, for it is in their conversion that the future of our world depends. Once we can enclose the body in a greater awareness of the soul's immortality, its desperate struggles for mere survival are subsumed under a concern for the spiritual development of the whole person. This is a truth that comes slowly to us as we confront the dissolution of the physical body as a part of the process of growth of the whole person into the way of immortality. 'In very truth I tell you, unless a grain of wheat falls into the ground and dies, it remains that and nothing more; but if it dies, it bears a rich harvest' (John 12.24). In this statement, the grain does not, of course, completely die, for if it did there could be no further development of any kind. In fact, the grain dies to its present form, and from its mutability, a minute shoot can emerge, the precursor of a plant immeasurably greater than the grain from which it originally sprung. The restraining elements of the grain are shed so that a new plant can develop from its heart, tiny as it is.

It seems profitable to regard the dying physical body in a rather similar light: its mortal elements are shed but from them a spiritual body emerges which encloses the soul in its onward journey. Of course, we are in the realms of mystery when we speculate thus, but St Paul does rather similarly when he writes: 'But, you may ask, how are the dead raised? In what kind of body? What stupid questions! The seed you sow does not come to life unless it has first died; and what you sow is not the body that shall be, but a bare grain, of wheat perhaps, or something else; and God gives it the body of his choice, each seed its own particular body. All flesh is not the same: there is human flesh, flesh of beasts, of birds and of fishes — all different. There are heavenly bodies and earthly bodies; and the splendour of the heavenly bodies is one thing, the splendour of the earthly another' (1 Corinthians 15.35–40). He goes on later to speak of the resurrection of the dead: what is sown as a perishable thing is raised imperishable. Sown in humiliation, it is raised in glory;

sown in weakness, it is raised in power; sown a physical body, it is raised a spiritual body (verses 42–44). He amplifies this by noting that flesh and blood can never possess the kingdom of God, the perishable cannot possess the imperishable (verse 50). St Paul no doubt wisely does not indicate the basis of this spiritual body. In the case of Jesus' resurrection body, I can envisage a direct transformation of his physical body to a spiritual body, but with us lesser mortals this is not the case: the physical body is laid to rest by interment or else cremated, in either event taking its place once more among the elements of the earth. What I personally believe constitute our own spiritual body are the thoughts, attitudes and aspirations that have formed the basis of our spiritual life while we were alive on earth. They have emanated from the physical body, and constitute the wedding clothes mentioned in Matthew 22.12, in connection with the guest invited to a wedding banquet (verses 1–14). If one sees the resurrection of the body that is mentioned in the Apostles' Creed in this type of light, it tells us how important is the life we lead while on earth in forming the body of the resurrected soul that is our identity in the shadowy realms of the after-life. The shadow refers to our poor understanding at the moment, not the state of the after-life, at least for those who lived in compassion and loving service while they were alive in the flesh.

I have explored this great mystery in some detail in order to allay the fears that we all, at least to some extent, share about the total extinction of the personality when the physical body is laid to rest. If we can see its great contribution to the life in eternity, that is here now as well as in the distant future, we need cling less obsessively to its ageing, disease-wracked substance and move on with greater equanimity to the immensity of life that is ours now, and will be even greater when we have shed the outer form and discovered the inner essence of our individual being. Having said all this, I would not like to give the impression that I despise the eternal value of matter, such as the substance of the physical body. The earth has its own life cycle and its evolutionary pattern, and St Paul in one of his greatest cosmic visions speaks of the hope of the universe itself being freed from the shackles of mortality and entering upon the glorious liberty of the children of

God (Romans 8.21). The spiritualization of matter is to me the most profound fulfilment of the doctrine of the resurrection of the body. With thoughts such as these in mind we can, at least to some extent, confront the moments of terror that wake us up in the middle of the night when we see only a golden youth behind us and the decrepitude of old age yawning menacingly in our shadow, the seeds of a misspent life pointing an accusing finger at our perennial selfishness.

The more positive aspect of our awareness of mortality is an acknowledgement that the present time is very important. Since no one knows when they may die, each of us should use what we have left as profitably as possible. In the end the only considerations that remain are love and forgiveness. It is wise to face our feelings of resentment and our innate prejudices that we regard as immutable truths with that sense of divine humour which sees the absurdity of so much of our attitudes in the light of eternity. Jesus advises us not to nurse anger against our brother, but to do all we can to come to terms with those who irritate and act against us, always remembering to put our own house in order and make peace with anyone who has a grievance against us, before presenting our gift at God's altar (Matthew 5.22–26). We cannot always effect a reconciliation, because the other person has likewise to play their part. Justice cannot simply be annulled, but there may be occasions when it has to be superseded by the finer action of loving forgiveness. Thus Jesus forgives those who effect his crucifixion because they are ignorant of the enormity of the crime they are committing (Luke 23.34). The religious elements are overcome with jealousy and fear, whilst the common people are easily misled: they expect a national hero, not one who suffers for the sins of the world.

If we are wise, we examine our motives and our reflex actions and attitudes with quiet deliberation, for most evil is committed when we think emotionally without due consideration of deeper issues. It is universal practice to make a final will in which we bequeath our possessions to those whose lives succeed our own, but few of us construct a mental testament, noting our grievances and shortcomings each day. This should be part of our daily recollectedness, for then we can start to put matters on a right footing in our spiritual ledger. We never know when death may call us to account, but even more important is the moment when we may truly start a new life in the immediate future. When we become wise, we recognize the propinquity of the new life and death. Thus I frequently tell those who come on retreat with me, that a retreat properly kept is a preparation for death, and I stress that this, far from being a morbid thought, should be an occasion for joyous release. In the silence of a retreat one can let go of many hindrances, experiencing life, perhaps for the first time, as pure uninhibited joy. I have little doubt that many of us will experience the transition of death in a similar manner. The release of past associations causes us immediate terror, just as Peter felt when he suddenly became aware of walking on insubstantial water. The presence of Christ reassured and supported him (Matthew 14.28–31).

And what happens when we are about to confront our own imminent death in stark reality? The intimations of the dark hours of the past now afflict us directly; we may, indeed almost certainly will, divert our full attention from the burning issue by consoling hopes that there may yet be a reprieve, that remarkable miracles have happened in the lives of people whom we know or have known in the past, therefore why not in ours also? In this way the unconscious dread is mollified by fully conscious hope. Soon there comes a reconciliation of this fearful juxtaposition: hope is broadened into a sweeping acceptance while fear is eased into a widening confidence in the process that is enveloping us as it has the countless numbers of others who preceded us in the strange, yet distantly known, journey of the soul to the promised land of rest prior to its next adventures. I have long been taught to compare the dying process with travelling on a swiftly moving escalator: our work is to stand upright and deliver ourselves with absolute confidence to the One who directs operations.

Of course, not all fear can be so easily disposed of as this. There is the fear of retribution after death for past sins; severely conventional religion, often pejoratively equated with orthodoxy, emphasizes this impending punishment and fills the dying person with mounting apprehension. I believe that God is love (1 John 4.16), and I cannot visualize, let alone accept, a love that punishes unceasingly, even if a temporary punishment may be necessary for the health and growth of the person, as taught in Proverbs 3.11–12. Therefore, as I have already said, the wise person keeps an account of their actions while they are still in fine health, for no one knows when death may strike. The fear of sudden death, as after an accident, stresses the acknowledgement of spiritual awareness in all our hearts, no matter how stridently our minds may deny an organizing process outside our little world of obsessive activity. If there is something that really hurts our conscience, it is wise to make a confession to someone in spiritual authority at once; absolution has a healing effect on the whole person. But one should avoid being scrupulous; none of us is perfect, and a sense of humour is at least as important as deep contrition, which, if persistent, indicates a psychological problem (with egoistical overtones) rather than spiritual sensitivity. The words of 1 John 3.19–20 are useful in this respect: 'This is how we shall know that we belong to the realm of truth, and reassure ourselves in his sight where conscience condemns us; for God is greater than our conscience and knows all.' Most priests know of penitents who go the rounds, also visiting the same confessor on a number of occasions with the same problem. The absolution they receive pours over them like water off a duck's back, because they are not really paying attention, their minds full of their own concerns rather than the word of God. The most that can be said in their favour is that this superficial conversation has a relieving effect, but unfortunately this does not last very long. Giving the last rites of a particular religious tradition is very much to be recommended, because these put the dying person's mind in the right attitude for what is about to befall it in the immediate period after the body's death. A confession is often very valuable in this situation.

In the case of the great majority of people the course of their lives has been illuminated with a surprising amount of naked courage in the face of really harrowing adversity. They themselves are far too modest to conceive this, let alone acknowledge it. It is hard to live completely virtuously in this world of shadow, so much under the influence of dark forces far beyond our knowledge, unless we are gifted with special sensitivity (frequently a very unpleasant gift, I need hardly add). But this spiritual struggle seems to be at the very heart of our incarnation. As Jesus says in admittedly very much higher authority, 'Now my soul is in turmoil, and what have I to say? "Father, save me from this hour"? No, it was for this that I came to this hour. Father, glorify your name' (John 12.27). This Gethsemane-like episode in John's Gospel indicates how closely linked are suffering and glorification. We too are called to actualize this glory that lies latent in all of us, the apparently insignificant (by the world's standards) no less than the phenomenally gifted. We achieve this by giving ourselves unconditionally to the present moment, so that the ego has been crucified on the cross of loving service and the Spirit of Truth can enter our soul and free the spirit within it. Then we can say with St Paul, 'I have been crucified with Christ: the life I now live is not my life, but the life which Christ lives in me' (Galatians 2.20).

When I consider the august subject of death, my mind invariably hearkens back to John Donne's beautiful sonnet.

Death, be not proud, though some have callèd thee
Mighty and dreadful, for thou art not so:
For those whom thou think'st thou dost overthrow
Die not, poor Death; nor yet canst thou kill me.

From Rest and Sleep, which but thy pictures be,
Much pleasure, then from thee much more must flow;
And soonest our best men with thee do go –
Rest of their bones and souls' delivery!

Thou'rt slave to fate, chance, kings, and desperate men,
And dost with poison, war, and sickness dwell;
And poppy or charms can make us sleep as well
And better than thy stroke. Why swell'st thou then?
   One short sleep past, we wake eternally,
   And Death shall be no more: Death, thou shalt die!

Yes indeed, the physical body departs from our earth in order to give space, nutriment and opportunity for those who follow on. But the soul moves on from glory to glory depending on the type of life it ordered while it worked within the limitations of its physical body. Death will be finally vanquished when we all travel from a carnal to a spiritual consciousness. Then the earth itself will be sanctified and enter into spiritual glory, while the living forms that once inhabited it will enter into the peace of God, with a little child leading the way.

12 The journey into truth

The McDonalds were a friendly couple whom I had known for about ten years. They had long ridden loosely to their inherited Anglican faith, having been deterred by a sequence of unsympathetic priests in the various parishes where circumstances had placed them. They were now pleasantly elderly, age often toning down extreme opinions whether social, political or religious, so that a previously inflammatory temperament now quietly relaxes in the shade as the soul reviews its previous earthly life and prepares unobtrusively for what is to follow. He was a retired accountant, while she had been kept busy with him and their four children. She was a fine amateur painter. These pleasant people had come on one of my retreats through enthusiastic recommendation by a friend, but they feared the silence that I required. At the end of the midweek retreat they emerged even more radiant than usual. They had discovered how a well-directed silence can draw a person to the very heart of their being, bringing many forgotten issues to the surface of consciousness, where they could be quietly confronted and dealt with, aided if necessary by the counselling skill of the conductor. I have already touched on the value of communicative silence. Nowhere is this shown to better advantage than in a retreat interview. In the friendly quietness many unattended issues can be discussed without tension. Not only did the McDonalds come to many other retreats, but they also flowed out to me in caring friendship, hoping in this way to repay me for the help I had been to them in retreat. Later they were to become fairly regular attenders at my church although they lived some distance out of London, forming part of the 'eclectic congregation' so typical of many central London churches.

When I visited their home I was introduced to their twin sons, Stephen and Roger (the other two children lived some distance away so that I rarely met them, but I learned that both, a son and a daughter, were happily married with two children each). Stephen and Roger were non-identical, a fact confirmed in their appearance and even more so in temperament; Stephen was a punctiliously correct, young solicitor with a delightful family of three small boys and a capable, compliant wife. Roger, by contrast, was always casually turned out, and unconventional in his way of life. He looked every inch the artist, and was in fact a talented painter, apparently inheriting some of the gift from his mother. He had a steady girl-friend whom he chose not to marry, and there was a lovely little daughter from their union. Stephen had been converted to a full Christian faith while at university; he was typically 'born again', contemptuous of the past faith that he had been taught, and imagining how best he could sacrifice himself for the benefit of his newly found faith. He found Roger's undisciplined style of living distasteful; that his niece had been born out of wedlock was a scandal and an insult to him. Roger for his part proclaimed a total atheism, and was never slow at tilting against the contradictions of organized religion with its unsavoury record of violence and repression of the human spirit. It was their mutual dogmatism that brought the two brothers closest together, even if the source of their assurance differed: religious enthusiasm in Stephen and a deliberately free life-style far removed from the norms of religious observance in Roger.

From all this one might have assumed that Stephen and I would have had much in common, while Roger would have been in continual conflict with me, but in fact the reverse was the case. Stephen found my broad spiritual sympathies, which extended to the great treasury of all the world faiths, extremely threatening, while Roger found in me a truly unusual Christian minister with whom he could discuss a variety of matters with complete openness. He enjoyed bantering me about the religious situation in Northern Ireland, where Christian groups were involved in terrible internecine strife. He also challenged me about the nature of a God who allowed various natural tragedies to torture the face of a planet he had allegedly made, one actually described as good in the opening chapter of the Book of Genesis. Much experience of the suffering inherent in life as well as my medical background allowed me to keep quiet and smile. I suggested that living in ardent dedication to the world reveals secrets of peculiar significance to the brave investigator. The pain of sensitive individuals causes them to enter into a scheme of purpose that leaves the purely scientific worker out in the cold. This was not a clean, convincing answer, but it at least left the way open for a further encounter in the struggle for meaning that is the basis of the human quest: suffering, destruction and final triumph as new life emerges from the ruins of the old. I doubt whether Roger grasped anything that I was saying, so satisfied was he with his painting and his little family.

Life did indeed progress pleasantly for the McDonald family. Stephen was fully occupied with his Christian youth group, to which he expended his weekend attention with unconditional commitment. Once, when his parents invited me to their home for two days, I found a small envelope addressed to me. It contained two texts: 'I am the way, the truth, and the life; no one comes to the Father except by me' (John 14.6); 'This Jesus is the stone, rejected by you the builders, which has become the corner-stone. There is no salvation through anyone else; in all the world no other name has been granted to mankind by which we can be saved' (Acts 4.11–12). It was signed by Stephen, who had the taste not to add to these texts with any personal comment. The implication was clear enough: I was not preaching the whole Gospel, but merely taking from it what pleased me. Furthermore I was fishing in decidedly murky waters by consorting even in the mind with other religious traditions. It was one thing to be aware of their menace, but quite another to show an affinity with some of their teachings. If Jesus is the Son of God, all other claims to divine knowledge are *ipso facto* erroneous. To Stephen's legal cast of mind this Aristotelian logic was impregnable. No one can attain salvation except by the Church. My way was wrong since it was syncretistic (forming a revised faith by including precepts from a number of religions) and eclectic (borrowing freely from various sources). I felt sad rather than offended, and I decided to ignore the criticism, not even revealing its contents to his parents, who by this time were fully of my cast of mind. Indeed, it was the freedom that my approach as well as my person offered that drew them close to me in bonds of the deepest affection.

And then tragedy struck with a mighty blow. Stephen noticed vague pains in his abdomen together with changed bowel habits. These he ignored, feeling that they were probably attacks of evil spirits intent on checking his spiritual work. A severe haemorrhage from the anus, however, made it clear even to him something was very amiss. He consulted his doctor who referred him to a surgeon; the diagnosis was clear enough: cancer of the lower part of the colon. This is one of the commonest malignancies in those of European stock, occurring most often in older people, but not always sparing even the young like Stephen, who was only in his early thirties. The tumour was excised expeditiously, but it was evident that it had already spread beyond the bounds of the bowel wall. The outlook was very poor, but he was given full doses of radiotherapy and chemotherapy. At the same time he was ministered to by his local charismatic prayer group, who were able to expel a number of evil spirits from him, including the spirit of cancer and the spirit of fear. Despite all this therapy, both medical and spiritual, the tumour spread rapidly. It was then that poor Stephen was afflicted by a terrible clinical depression, probably the combined effect of the chemotherapy and feelings of guilt that he had failed to respond to the prayers and ministrations of his Christian friends. The depression mercifully responded rapidly to the usual antidepressant therapy.

It was at this stage that Stephen asked desperately to see me. When I visited him, I found him in floods of tears. These were not the outcome of his depression so much as his regret for treating me so discourteously in the past. He had, as it were, suddenly seen the light, for new impressions and considerations had poured into his mind in the course of his own fearful passion, comparable in its way to that of his Master, Jesus Christ. He apologized profusely to me for the bad thoughts he had harboured against me in the past, and wanted to discuss the deepest spiritual matters with me. He had already come round to a much more catholic view of the spiritual life, that the heart is a better measure of sanctity than the beliefs held in the mind, and that sanctity is not related so much to the religious denomination of people as to their inner lives, which in turn are reflected in the loving service rendered to their fellows. I discovered that he knew this in his deepest intuition long before his present trial, but was won over to the born-again position because of the conviction of salvation that it provided. Dogmatic systems of belief, whether centred on the higher religions or the numerous cults that infest the mental climate of our age, gain converts who are inwardly uncertain of God's love. They are liable to respond to the proffered affection of group members ('love-bombing' is the technical term), and so be drawn ever more deeply into a human-made morass until their sense of discernment and free will are dangerously vitiated.

I saw Stephen weekly, first in hospital and later in my own flat, which he appreciated for its tranquillity and inner glow. The zenith of a rapidly mounting climax of spiritual understanding was reached when he wrote quite spontaneously to me: 'Now I understand the meaning of those two texts I left with you on that fateful day. The essential I that is the way, the truth, and the life, and without which no one can come to the Father is none other than love. Anyone who knows a love that is prepared to sacrifice itself to the end is inspired by the Spirit of Christ no matter what the person may call themselves in terms of a denomination. There is indeed no salvation except by this love. I know that such love is personified in the being of Jesus, but who am I to deny that it is demonstrated by the holy ones among the Jews, Muslims, Hindus, Buddhists, Sikhs, and those of other faiths? And even those who refuse to acknowledge the living God while showing his love in the world are also in the halls of salvation. When I think of all the cruelty inflicted by Christians over the centuries both among themselves and on those of other faiths, I cannot believe that their kind either know Christ or follow in his foot-steps. I thank God for my cancer in opening my mind to a truth that was completely hidden from me in the days of my worldly success and complacency.' Stephen died a few days after making this confession to me. This experience was a revealing chapter in my life no less than his, for it explained to me the fascination of religious fundamentalism even among highly intelligent people whom one might have thought would know better. The heart may indeed be a more reliable measure of spiritual truth than the mind, but its findings must invariably be tested by the reason lest enthusiasm obfuscates discernment and leads one desperately astray. In the end it is the intuition that is the provider of the finest discernment. One remembers once more the four personality functions of thinking, feeling, sensation and intuition mentioned in Chapter 5.

I was privileged to officiate at Stephen's funeral, which drew an impressive congregation, and then to conduct the brief service in the crematorium which was reserved for his family and very close friends. At the end of this service I was accosted by Roger, who was in a very different mood from that of the usual teasing banter of previous occasions. He was very angry as he asked me, 'Why did this bloody God of yours allow Stephen to die like that? Why didn't he choose me instead?' The implication was obvious: why did a decent person like Stephen die while a bounder like Roger was spared? The answer poured out of my mouth without any prior thought: 'Because he was worthier than you.' Roger simply glared at me in uncomprehending fury, then he turned away and joined his family. I myself was amazed at my answer to his question, for it came directly from the Holy Spirit who inspires my numerous sermons in church and my retreat addresses. I know this because I do not prepare what I am to say, but simply let the words flow from my lips.

After Stephen's death the McDonalds withdrew more and more into themselves, but they continued to come to my church from time to time. Age was beginning to take its toll in the form of osteo-arthritis and eye problems. Eventually they retired to Dorset near one of their other children. I heard that Roger had proceeded with a civil marriage. I suspect this was in honour of Stephen's memory, for he so disapproved of the unstable position of the little girl born of a common-law wife. Roger continued to wrestle with a God who let the side down so often, and he would not join any religious denomination. I have continued to salute Roger's integrity, often feeling closer to his position than that of many bigoted believers. But in the end an atheistic stance is quite impossible for me.

A search for truth is integral to the human condition. The human has investigated the universe from the minutest elementary particle to the furthest galaxies. The mystery of life has been reduced to nucleic acids and genes. Technology has become the basis of communication in our computer age. But the basis of life still eludes us, as does the fate of the individual when the physical body dies. There is compelling evidence of the survival of the inner being, or soul, of the individual, but scientific proof is still not available. Throughout the period of evolution of *Homo sapiens* from its most primitive human ancestors there is evidence of religious rites among the remains found in caves. With the advent of civilizations religion has developed with the appearance of spiritual geniuses, especially in Asia, stretching from the Middle East to China. And now there are a number of higher religions which are well represented in the world we inhabit. Each in its own way has tackled the enigma of life, suffering, death and purpose. None is completely satisfying to the uncommitted seeker, but each seems to stress some universal truth of the human condition.

There is a difference between spirituality and religion; the first is the pursuit for the vision of God, whereas the second is the detailed path set out for that pursuit. In this respect the word God implies a personal deity, but an alternative term that reveals the absolute being is also acceptable. We are all, I believe, endowed with some awareness of the divine being, and spirituality gives itself to bringing this awareness fully within our reach. Its way is essentially one of self-renunciation, the fruits of which, unimaginable until the quest is begun, are a discovery of a deeper self which is in eternal communion with the divine nature and therefore also with the true selves of all our human peers, and an increasing affinity with creation itself. This is the way of the mystic which we shall consider again in Chapter 14. The path towards this ultimate knowledge may be traversed intuitively by the mystic (and I believe mystical awareness is a property of the human soul, but apparently far better developed in some souls than in others), but for those of us who are more materially based with only a glimpse of a higher realm of existence, a definite path of spiritual progress is necessary. This has been provided by the spiritual geniuses already mentioned, and it forms the basis of a religion.

In itself religion is a fine thing, but the multiplicity of living faiths is bound to provide a stumbling-block for a believer. Which is the true one? The answer is, to my mind, pragmatic; in other words, the claims to authority of any faith are proved by the practical results which are seen in the believer. 'You will recognize them by their fruit' (Matthew 7.16). As Portia puts it to her waiting-woman Nerissa in *The Merchant of Venice* (Act 1, scene 2, 11–15), 'If to do were as easy as to know what were good to do, chapels had been churches, and poor men's cottages princes' palaces. It is a good divine that follows his own instructions; I can easier teach twenty what were good to be done, than be one of the twenty to follow mine own teaching.' In practice we follow our ancestral faith (or lack of it); in the modern world secular education weans many from it to a convenient agnosticism, but in fact it is the general lack of spirituality among those who profess that faith, including the ordained ministers, whose example of love, honesty and general integrity are crucial in influencing the young, that depresses and eventually repels the society around them. I would imagine that Roger McDonald's adamant atheism was due in no small measure to the examples he encountered in his church school. By contrast Stephen had a better developed awareness of the numinous (a combined feeling of awe and attraction characteristic of the human sense of communion with God), but he had not known the self-eclipsing joy of the mystic. This was to be his fortune only shortly before his death. Thus Stephen's spirituality could keep him in his religious observance despite the unspiritual nature of his school, whereas Roger, in the same ambience, threw the whole 'God thing' up as illusory.

Some of us convert from one denomination to another in our inherited faith and a few move decisively from one faith to another. I think that this movement is often pre-ordained, the individual working in the newly found religion much more happily than in the old one. Another equally spiritually active person may make the reverse movement for the same reasons. We all have to learn the telling lesson that a religion *per se* will not change our characters, especially if we begin to idolize it to the detriment of other faiths. Mystics, though loyally identifying with a particular faith, know in their heart that all the great religions are alternative ways of reaching the essential vision of God, no matter how this may be apprehended by the theologians of various faiths. We all long for the ultimate truth, something far beyond rational definition. Thus the 'rich young man' whom we have mentioned so often asks Jesus what he should do to win eternal life. His mode of life was clearly spotless, but his one weakness was his dependence on material possessions. Would his quest for ultimate truth lead him to sell everything he had, giving the proceeds to the poor, and then follow the simple life of Jesus and his disciples? He could not make that final renunciation, much to his consternation. Jesus then makes the unforgettable comparison of a camel passing through the eye of a needle more easily than a rich man entering the kingdom of God (Mark 10. 17–27). If one considers this telling episode less gloomily, one can see that the rich man had not yet reached that degree of spiritual development that would have allowed him to renounce material possessions. Maybe he would have been able to do so later on, perhaps after some severe tragedy had forcibly removed some of his wealth from him, or else a sad bereavement of a dearly loved one which would have exposed the futility of riches. At the end of this story Jesus reminds us that what is impossible for humans is fully possible for God. In other words, the divine assistance can allow any of us to perform 'supernatural' deeds.

This consideration explains my own Christian commitment without in any way looking down on any of the other great traditions. In Christ I see the complete confluence of the human and the divine: two natures in one person. And through him I can see how the corrupt human nature can be changed until it is sanctified, becoming holy in the very image of God. The change is a pure gift of God, the divine grace. All that is required of us is openness to that gift, a virtue that is called faith in the context of complete trust, such as a small child would possess but a sophisticated adult would be unable to comprehend. While we cling to material aids, as did the rich young man, we cannot accommodate the divine grace, and usually we are changed by some outer circumstance that causes our pride to yield. At that moment a new life opens to us as it did to Saul of Tarsus on the road to Damascus, as described in the ninth chapter of the Acts of the Apostles. It is this transforming capacity of Christ which I see as the key to the emergence of a new humanity.

But like all other divine revelations, the work is left in human hands. Soon it becomes institutionalized into the form of a religious body, the Church, and then the politics of power supersede the grace of God. The corruption of Christianity by the power of various religious bodies is possibly the supreme tragedy of the world; how so much promise has been betrayed and annulled by those who call themselves Christians, yet seem to be devoid of the Spirit of Christ in their dealings with their fellow humans and indeed the whole creation! But the transforming work continues despite the unworthiness of its protagonists. Certainly the worldwide civilization that is the product of Christian social concern and education cannot be denied; taken in conjunction with its mother religion Judaism, it has indeed turned the world upside-down with the hope of a real paradise when the dark shadow has been finally expunged from human consciousness. Our present century has seen some of this terrifying work in progress, but the outlook is good provided we all lose ourselves in Christian service which is not afraid to give up its very life for the created whole. I cannot with all humility see any of the other world faiths rising to this vision of completeness in the historical order. Jesus told his disciples, 'In the world you will have suffering. But take heart! I have conquered the world' (John 16.33). This seems to me to be the cosmic truth whose inspiration we are all called on to embrace. Then the Church will be synonymous with humanity at large.

After this intense consideration of spiritual insights and truths, my mind goes back to Stephen in the throes of his death agony which was also an introduction to the new life. Henry Vaughan's poem 'Peace' speaks highly to my condition.

My soul there is a country
  Far beyond the stars,
Where stands a wingèd sentry
  All skilful in the wars,
There above noise, and danger
  Sweet peace sits crowned with smiles,
And one born in a manger
  Commands the beauteous files.
He is thy gracious friend,
  And (O my soul awake!)
Did in pure love descend
  To die here for thy sake,
If thou canst get but thither,
  There grows the flower of peace,
The rose that cannot wither,
  Thy fortress, and thy ease;
Leave then thy foolish ranges;
  For none can thee secure,
But one, who never changes,
  Thy God, thy life, thy cure.

The winged sentry is the archangel Michael. 'Then war broke out in heaven; Michael and his angels fought against the dragon' (Revelation 12.7). The dragon and his angels were too weak, and they lost their place in heaven. The dragon was thrown down, that ancient serpent who led the whole world astray, whose name is the Devil, or Satan; he was thrown down to the earth, and his angels with him. So continues this account of war in heaven, a useful point of departure for what now follows.

13 The confluence of darkness and light

In Chapter 3 I spoke of my psychic nature; it is a universal property of all living beings, but in the human it is given the capacity to become articulate, subject to analysis by the intellect and given to others as a part of social intercourse. We communicate physically by means of the five senses, intellectually through the mind and the reasoning faculty, and directly in a way that transcends both physical sensation and reason through the medium of the soul. In this mode of communication the term 'psychic' finds its logical, practical and most accurate usage. Like physical and intellectual communication, it may be used selfishly or beneficially for society as a whole; communication in itself is morally neutral, its use being completely subject to the person themself. But whereas physical and intellectual communication is at least partly under the control of the will, the psychic dimension is essentially a function of the unconscious aspect of the mind, and is very much linked to the intuition. It is like the workings of the Holy Spirit described by Jesus to Nicodemus in John 3.8, 'The wind blows where it wills; you hear the sound of it, but you do not know where it comes from or where it is going. So it is with everyone who is born from the spirit.' It is not surprising that psychic communication lies beyond scientific measurement, so that many investigators refuse to acknowledge its existence. And yet its products impinge sufficiently on the lives of many normal people to make its existence a reality, sometimes beneficial and on other occasions a great nuisance and even extremely frightening. If like me one is very attuned psychically, a range of experience is one's gift (and also sometimes one's lot), a gift which may completely separate oneself from many other people who appear to be deliberately obtuse to modalities of existence other than the crudely material. It was this sensitivity that so separated me even from my parents, especially my father, for I believe my mother had this sensitivity in her but was afraid to face its consequences in the midst of the very comfortable life she was able to lead.

Some psychic experiences are emotionally neutral, like those in which the future is suddenly revealed (precognition) or a past event sensed in a particular locality (retrocognition). There may be an unaccountable transference of information from one mind to another (telepathy) or a sudden vision of an event occurring elsewhere (clairvoyance). The first two experiences are of a time shift, whereas the second two involve the present transmission of information in a non-rational manner. If there is an emotional response, this is due to the information received, sometimes pleasant, sometimes unpleasant, and often merely of general interest. Many psychic experiences are frightening inasmuch as they bring an atmosphere of gloom or vicious destruction with them. Sometimes there are bizarre physical phenomena such as the sound of moving furniture, footsteps or heavy breathing together with the unaccountable disappearance of objects from their usual sites, and faults in the electrical system. All these constitute the familiar poltergeist (which means a noisy mischievous spirit), which is typically seen in connection with adolescents whose sexual energy is not properly channelled and then expresses itself in the form of psychical phenomena. In my experience a similar type of effect can also be produced by the unquiet spirits of the dead, which still remain earth-bound instead of moving to the vaster realms of the after-life where God will receive them for further training. Often they want to proceed, but are stopped by a sense of guilt for unsavoury actions in their past earth life. The phenomena they produce, whether physical or emotional, are SOS signals, and once they are absolved, they move on quite rapidly. The unquiet dead often produce feelings of dread or evil, and are usually, in my experience, dealt with quite easily by direct conversation and explanation of their situation. Sometimes a young child or an aborted foetus may remain earth-bound, and will cause trouble to their family through ignorance and possibly resentment also. Again I have found that they are easily sent on their way; some ministers of deliverance use a Requiem Mass instead, but I have not found it necessary except in a few cases. I prefer the concept of deliverance to exorcism, since I deliver the entity or spirit to God's care and do not merely expel it from its present abode.

I have included this consideration of psychic phenomena and the ministry of deliverance as an introduction to something much more pertinent to the subject of mood paintings: demonic activities. At present my work in delivering demonic spirits from the world of living forms, in other words our own domain, to God's care is paramount in my ministry. I have both witnessed the effects such infestations can have in the environment of the demonic activity and also known only too well at first hand the influence it can have on me. It is necessary first to define the nature of the demonic, and this requires an understanding of the angelic hierarchy. Angels are essentially messengers of God; they bring the divine assistance down to humans and other living forms on our earth, and no doubt elsewhere too in our enormous cosmos, the combined universe and the forms outside the Godhead itself (which include the Communion of Saints and the ministry of angels). I believe we each have our own guardian angel who protects us by warning us of incipient trouble or imminent danger; usually we are far too preoccupied with our own affairs to take notice of a warning that comes from the intuition (the way by which the psychic field is mediated), but sometimes we may be aware and co-operate accordingly.

Angelic activity as such is always beneficial, but there is also a race of fallen angels, who are under the control of their master, whom we call Satan, Lucifer or the devil – whether these three are identical or closely related members of the highest echelon of darkness is debatable, but the distinction is not important from our point of view. Legend speaks of the fall of Lucifer, God's favourite angel who took power on itself without the prior sanction of God. The angel fell, precipitating a pre-mundane Fall which prefigured the Fall of humanity as described in Genesis 3. All this, including Genesis 3, is mythological (spiritual truth described symbolically), but a wise person does not summarily dismiss it as nonsense.

The work of the devil is the destruction of all that exists; it is the enemy of the Creator whom we call God. Like Iago in Shakespeare's *Othello*, it starts by putting destructive emotions like fear and suspicion into the human mind, so that in the end the most abominable crimes are committed for the most plausible reasons. The servants of the devil, the demonic spirits, carry forward its destructive potential. But it must always be emphasized that no psychic incursion can affect an immaculate human mind; there is always a serious flaw in the person that permits demonic invasion and perversion. This is most important, otherwise all manner of atrocities, like the Nazi Holocaust, could simply be ascribed to demonic activity in wholly innocent humans. In the above-mentioned example Hitler was a willing medium, full of hatred, for the dark forces of the devil to possess him, and through him to attack and captivate the German people. It is appalling to think of possibly the most civilized nation in the world following so effortlessly the call of demonic fury, until one remembers the pride of a people, aware of their brilliance, brought low by their defeat in the First World War and the terrible consequences that later followed as part of the Great Depression of the later twenties and early thirties of our century. They turned to Hitler as a last resort, and were captivated by his message of racial purity with the consequent elimination of alien groups that polluted the blood-stream of the great Germanic people. How easy it was for the demonic spirits to move in and work in collaboration with the aroused populace intent on revenge and utter destruction of all it had learned to hate! If one ponders on this terrible tragedy it is evident that the German people bore the principal responsibility for the Holocaust, but that they were admirably assisted by the devil's messengers.

This being the case, it could be reasonably argued, 'Why bring in the devil at all?' This important objection introduces the pertinence of Occam's Razor, which argues in effect that circumstances should be pruned of unnecessary additions. If a person's destructive actions can be attributed to their moral deficiency or mental ill-health, there is no need to bring in demons from outer space. Speaking from my own experience, the two qualities that would arouse my suspicion would be the intensity of the destructiveness and the aura of evil around the individual. These two are best assessed by one with strong psychic sensitivity; women are often more aware that something is amiss on a demonic level than men, who tend to be limited by their intellectual judgement. In other words the case is one of intuition versus reason. In everyday life both have to be satisfied, for intuition, if unchecked, can acquire an emotional strangle-hold and precipitate superstition on the one hand and fanaticism on the other. This is where born-again believers, whom we considered in the last chapter, can come seriously amiss. It has been my saving grace to be both intellectually gifted and psychically sensitive; my medical training was clearly no error on the part of the One who has guided my life. I only wish that I could collaborate with a sympathetic psychiatrist in some of my work; both of us would benefit by the exchange of understanding. I have little doubt that mentally disturbed people are more open to demonic attack just as, on another level, are those who dabble in the occult and those involved in satanism.

In my experience, when an individual is demonically infested, by which I mean that the evil spirit is close to the personality but does not possess it, there is a terrible depression together with suicidal thoughts and suspicion levelled at those people close in family relationship or friendship. Psychiatrically this mimics a depression with paranoid features, but the person was previously well and the attack is sudden and associated with an awareness of great evil. This terrifies the victim and their associates. While there may indeed be a frankly psychological component to such a case, I can sense the demonic element. This I command to leave the person and proceed to that place in the life beyond death which God has prepared for its reception and healing. I believe that the authority of my priesthood and the spiritual power that accompanies it is vital in this work, but it would not ring true if I were merely to repeat words like a formula while having no real contact with the demonic spirit. I am able to tell inwardly whether my work has succeeded or not, but I confirm this by the tossing of a coin that I have blessed. When I ask the question I arrange that heads are positive and tails negative. This test should show a minimal influence from my own thoughts or prejudices, and indeed the answer given is often disappointing inasmuch as my work has been fruitless and I have to start again. I never initiate this coin test except after saying the Lord's Prayer and then the well-known Anglican Collect, 'Almighty God, forasmuch as without thee we are not able to please thee, mercifully grant that thy Holy Spirit may in all things direct and rule our hearts, through Jesus Christ our Lord. Amen.' In other words, the whole process of deliverance is conducted in a spirit of rapt prayer, so that one's own consciousness is illuminated by the prayer from on high. An individual not adept at prayer should never approach this dangerous ministry, for one is indeed in danger of demonic attack oneself. It is imperative to work with another person who is equally attuned psychically and and has a living Christian faith. I have little doubt that the name of Jesus has a specially powerful effect in protecting us from evil. Jesus himself was an expert at deliverance work. Unfortunately this combination of psychic sensitivity and Christian commitment is not very common, as I learned when the person with whom I had worked for over twelve years died in 1993. She was ninety-three years old, and was active until the time of a massive stroke that killed her after ten days' gallant fight. So far I have found no replacement, and a very wise friend has told me that I never shall; God alone will be my protector now. I also believe that my friend is helping me from the realms far beyond our knowledge.

When a locality is demonically infested there is a general atmosphere of gloom. Many disasters befall the place with accidents and tragedies of various types. When deliverance is performed there is often a speedy return to more pleasant conditions. I am, as one schooled in scientific research, well aware that a favourable outcome is not a proof that a particular hypothesis is correct; it might have been a coincidence, the improvement occurring in any event. When a number of similar cases show the same pattern, one is on stronger ground, but the sceptic will think of any alternative to the demonic one, so

ingrained are many people's prejudices against psychical phenomena. In any case my work is not so much to convert people to
my beliefs as to bring relief to those who are oppressed. I believe
that in due course the type of sensitivity that I know will be
widely disseminated.

When I am attacked demonically I usually awake from a
peculiar type of dream that I alluded to in Chapter 11. I am
carried back over many years and remember old friends and
colleagues. As I slowly come out of the memory I find that they
are probably dead, while I am much older than I was in the
dream. A sense of agitation comes over me with undertones of
mounting fear. This fear is one of total extinction, and if I do
nothing about it, I am insidiously carried forward into the
beginning of a severe depression. I have learned to stem the
process at once by getting out of bed, praying, and then carrying
out the deliverance sequence similar to what I have already
described. I always bring my dead friend into the work, believing
that she too is under some attack. The main fact is that the attack
is rapidly curbed, and I can return relieved to my bed. If the
experience has occurred in the early hours, I will remain awake
for some time, my mind being understandably active but
fortunately in a positive mood. After about an hour or so I will
fall asleep, and wake up fresh later on. Sometimes I have a rather
similar attack only a short time before I usually rise, in which
case I rest after the deliverance, but do not fall asleep again. What
I have described differs from the common nightmare, of which it
is clearly a species, in that it can progress to a clinical depression
if not checked at once. I can see now that one aspect of my
depressive tendency has been related to demonic attacks that I
have suffered for a long time. Until I became actively involved in
the deliverance ministry, I was powerless to check these depressions at their earliest stage by removing the offending agents.
Now at least I am able to cope with one cause of my depressive
tendency. Psychically sensitive people are very open to demonic
attack, but at least they can repel it if they understand what is
happening to them.

Vulnerability is the price we pay for participating in relationships. Harking back to Martin Buber's dictum that all real living

is meeting, we cannot live properly in complete seclusion even if the pain inherent in communion is avoided. When we relate to our fellows there is sorrow as well as joy; inasmuch as death is our common end, the grief of bereavement must terminate even the closest of earthly ties. What makes a relationship beautiful or detestable is the psychic rapport or repulsion that exists between the two (or more) parties. A person with strong psychic sensitivity can relate especially well to other people; they are natural counsellors. But if their character is evil, they can emanate destructive emotions to others, and cause much trouble. Sometimes such a person is unaware of the harm they are causing, but on other occasions they are acting quite deliberately. This is an aspect of 'black magic'. In my view it is wrong to attempt influencing others by psychic means, even if one really does have the faculty to do so and one's objectives are completely honourable. There is One alone who may do this; we aid God by our intercessions, not by assuming his powers. When one intercedes properly one simply allows the love of God to flow to the person for whom one is praying. The two great command-ments are to love God and to love our neighbour as ourself (Mark 12.29–31). Love entails giving our very life to God's command and our neighbour's service; it does not mean dominating anyone. Therefore I am unsympathetic to all magic, 'white' (allegedly beneficial) as well as 'black'.

When there are malign psychic links between one person and another, it is my work to break them in the power of God. This is not difficult provided the victim really wants to break connec-tion with the person causing the trouble. As in everything else, free will is not to be bypassed or disregarded, for little real heal-ing will occur until all give their unqualified support. When there is communication between the dead and the living, once again it is the psychic function of the soul that is involved. While I, following the deuteronomic prohibition against trying to contact the dead (Deuteronomy 18.11, also Leviticus 19.31), discounte-nance the work of mediums in striving to effect communication between the living and the dead (I make an exception in the case of genuine psychical research involving qualified parapsycho-logists), I know from my own experience that the dead can quite

spontaneously communicate with the living. This communication is not by any means fatuous, but is effected for a definite
purpose; quite often in my experience to give useful advice.
Sometimes the message is simply one of continued life and caring
after death has closed one chapter of a relationship. To me the
resurrection appearances of Jesus to his disciples (but never his
antagonists during the forty days up to the Ascension) were
primarily to assure them of his love and forgiveness despite their
despicable behaviour during his passion. They were then
renewed in their faith – in fact resurrected – and ready for the
immense work ahead of them. It is this matter of communication
with the dead that has given the word 'psychic' such a bad
reputation among many believers, but it should be recognized
that the psychic dimension is much vaster than this one murky
area. Indeed without it we could hardly communicate as feeling,
creative people. We would be more like highly evolved computers than human beings!

Although the unquiet dead usually pose no problems of
frightening evil, I have to describe one case where the reverse was
true. It involved a young woman who disappeared in mysterious
circumstances and was never seen alive again. I was called to a
maximum security prison to interview a long-term prisoner who
had been playing with a ouija-board in his cell. He was obviously
psychically sensitive, for he had picked up a communicator who
claimed to be this woman in person. I tried to separate her from
the medium, but in vain. I also tried to break the psychic links
between the two, but again fruitlessly. All this happened towards
the end of 1990, when the Gulf crisis was culminating in war.
Soon after 1991 began I developed a familiar depressive episode,
heralded by the usual insomnia; I have little doubt that the
general atmosphere of gloom at least helped to precipitate this
severe attack. It was only moderately responsive to antidepressants, not so satisfactorily as in the earlier attack I described in
Chapter 1. Then one morning in mid-Lent I was awakened at
about 6.30 a.m. by an encounter I shall never forget. It was as if a
being from outer space had landed on my soul, for a time
obfuscating my general consciousness so that I was not in full

control of my feelings. But this soon calmed down, the depression unfortunately being conspicuously worse and having a component of anger that was unlike the previous episode or my general demeanour. The one symptom that was paramount was an absolute insomnia, even going to sleep was difficult, and once awake there was no chance of returning to sleep. Even very high doses of the antidepressant had absolutely no effect on the insomnia. Fortunately it responded well to a powerful hypnotic (sleeping drug), the effect lasting two or even three days. My mood was most unpleasant, an amalgam of despondency, anger, and hopelessness, and I looked ill and older than my years. Nevertheless I continued my church duties without demur, and my counselling work did not appear to suffer, if the response of my clients was anything to trust. It was especially of interest that I preached the 'Seven Last Words on the Cross' on Good Friday from noon to 3 p.m. (as I do each year) with a brilliance that startled me. I have no reason to doubt that this preaching marathon impressed the congregation also.

After Easter Day I took a break in the country for a week, but there was no change in my depression. On the Friday of the following week a small charismatic prayer group met in my flat – we alternated between a monastery and my flat on a monthly basis – and this time there were only three of us: a police officer who is as psychic as I, an elderly lady who is rather deaf and myself. Much of the time was involved in petitions to God, and I prayed fervently that my depression might lift (as I had done repeatedly in my own private prayer time). At the end of the hour the meeting broke up with the Lord's Prayer, and then the police officer, a great friend of mine, asked me if I had done a recent exorcism in my flat because he sensed a dead person around. At the time I could not recall such an exorcism, but one thing was certain: the depression was lifting fast and my absolute insomnia had broken. Nevertheless it did not completely disappear, for I still needed a small dose of antidepressant each night before retiring, if I was to have a good sleep.

For the next year I had to continue taking the small dose of antidepressant, but I knew that this was not simply a matter of dependence, or addiction, since these drugs do not create this problem. At that time a parishioner of mine, a lady psychiatrist and psychoanalyst, invited me to dinner. Afterwards I recounted this intriguing story to her, but very soon her two cats leapt out of the room and ran away as far as they could in the closed house, for the weather was still cold. At last I was able to put two and two together. The cats had sensed the presence of an unquiet spirit, which I had brought into close contact with me by discussing its case in the way I did. When I arrived in my flat I telephoned my 'deliverance partner', the aged lady whom I have already mentioned, and we 'looked in' together – we did all our work over the telephone since she lived in Wells, which is about 150 miles from London. Sure enough the unquiet spirit was still there. I commanded it to proceed to God's healing and care in the usual way. The next day I said a Requiem Mass for it. At the end of the Mass I was sure that the spirit of this unfortunate woman was at last at peace, and I very soon was able to dispense with the antidepressant altogether.

This remarkable case had a further flare-up a few months ago (in 1994), when I recounted its details to another highly psychic woman doctor working with Jungian therapy. At once she was aware of a hostile presence in the sitting-room of her house with something grabbing her right wrist. I assured her that all was well, and then proceeded to dispel this powerful thought form. I suspect that the murdered woman (I have little doubt that this is how she met her end) was grabbed in this way prior to being killed by her assailant. Interestingly, the two doctors and the murdered woman lived in the same area of London. It is evident to me that the events leading up to her death were unsavoury, and this is why her spirit remained unquiet. The mediumistic prisoner was able to locate and befriend her, as I was then to do. She required my body so much that she actually possessed it during the period of my blackest depression. I often think of Sydney Carter's well-known hymn 'Lord of the Dance'. In the fourth verse runs the line, 'It's hard to dance with the devil on your back'. Only Jesus could do this, but I at least know what it feels like to have an unquiet spirit on my back and still continue my dance of counselling and preaching even in a Good Friday setting. It was the prayer in the intimate charismatic circle that released her (and me also), but she was still close to me. Only later did I understand the full nature of the case, and then could easily deliver her to God's care. I suspect guilt played a part in holding her back to this earth and away from God's unconditional love. The police officer assures me that the likelihood of finding her remains after a period of nearly ten years is remote in the extreme. However I am content with St Paul's reminder in Romans 12.19, 'Vengeance is mine, says the Lord, I will repay'.

I hope that this rather lurid drama may remind therapists of the future that we are all parts of the one body of humanity, and that the psychic interdependence that this entails can easily be reflected in severe mood changes that one person can implant on another. When we can fully grasp this, it could be that psychology, to say nothing of psychiatry, may make a quantum leap into a new century.

14 Recognition

Who are we? Mere clods of matter, here today and destined for the grave tomorrow? Psychic entities whose influence is wafted a distance away, and then diluted with a fresh wind of oblivion, here today and gone tomorrow? Creatures of vain pretension striving for the moon and pushing our way ahead, only to find that our destination is extinction as others push their way ahead of us? Job puts it more poetically: 'Every being born of a woman is short-lived and full of trouble. He blossoms like a flower and withers away; fleeting as a shadow, he does not endure; he is like a wineskin that perishes or a garment that moths have eaten' (Job 14.1–2). The Psalmist writes: 'You turn mortals back to dust, saying, "Turn back, you children of mortals", for in your sight a thousand years are as the passing of one day or as a watch in the night. You cut them off; they are asleep in death. They are like grass which shoots up; though in the morning it flourishes and shoots up, by evening it droops and withers' (Psalm 90.3–6). Another view is expressed thus: 'Lord, let me know my end and the number of my days; tell me how short my life is to be. I know you have made my days a mere span long, and my whole life is as nothing in your sight. A human being, however firm he stands, is but a puff of wind' (Psalm 39.4–5). Even the very glowing Psalm 103 has this to say about the human condition: 'The days of a mortal are as grass; he blossoms like a wild flower in the meadow: a wind passes over him, and he is gone, and his place knows him no more' (Psalm 103.15–16). However, the passage continues much more radiantly: 'But the Lord's love is for ever on those who fear him, and his righteousness on their posterity,

on those who hold fast to his covenant, who keep his command-
ments in mind' (verses 17–18). Yes indeed, the human condition
is one of perishable matter endowed with immortality by the
Spirit of God: a spiritual animal with feet on the earth and a head
in the clouds.

The work of the human is to sanctify the world, to endue it
with a radiance that shows the uncreated light of God's presence
in every creature, and to lift it all up to God as the tortured body
of Jesus rose in an undreamed-of revelation on the third day after
its crucifixion to the glory of a resurrection body that altered the
course of history. All this sounds melodramatic and purely
visionary, but the way is both more mundane and more
profound. When we think about ourselves, our ultimate futility
becomes frighteningly apparent, as the three texts quoted above
confirm. But when we lose ourselves in fruitful activity, activity
in which we give of ourselves unsparingly yet joyfully to the
world around us, we surmount our circumscribed ego consciousness and enter a world of communication that soon matures into
communion, or fellowship. We are told in the Bible to love our
neighbour as ourself (Luke 10.27, based on Leviticus 19.18). We
begin to love our neighbour when we lose an awareness of our
own separation by giving freely to that neighbour, who, in our
global world, is everybody and indeed the whole created order.
As we lose ourselves as separate units, so we begin to find out
who we really are in the economy of the whole, which includes
not merely our world or even the vast universe, but the entire
cosmos with its saints on high and its ministering angels. This
enormous range of fellowship comes to us when we serve with
joyous intent; we learn that we love ourselves as part of the
created order, in which our own particular sins and vices are
swallowed up in a love so all-embracing that we quite literally
forget what is past and strive with all our strength to bring the
love of God into the present situation. This is the way in which
the artist and scientist are carried along by the creative impulse
that will never be satisfied until the masterpiece is created or new
insights are encountered in understanding the mechanism of the
world and the workings of the universe. We lesser people who
cannot claim any special artistic genius or scientific knowledge

can attain that same degree of selflessness by getting on quietly and efficiently with our work of service to those around us and leaving all self-centred actions behind us. If we give ourselves fully to the work of loving service, we will find in that experience an identity that is inseparable from all creation. This is the experience known to the mystic in the moment of illumination when they are lifted up above their surroundings, and enter into the uncreated light of God where all that is created is found to be a mere fragment of divine reality. And yet each living element is not only represented but is also identified with the whole.

This is who we really are: the physical body does indeed die and its elements return to the earth from which they were fashioned, but the essential being, which we call the soul, enters into the realm of divine unity, depending on its ability to face the physically blinding but intellectually illuminating uncreated light of God, the same that Saul of Tarsus (later St Paul) encountered on the road of Damascus (Acts 9.3–9). In those of evil lineage, the soul retires to the darkness of hell, whereas the saint's soul passes effortlessly to the light of paradise. Most of us proceed to the intermediary zone of purgatory.

In the end we realize that we do indeed love our neighbour as ourself, because the neighbour is ourself, not in physical identity but in corporate union. In that love the various invidious character traits which make everyday relationships so painful are healed of their selfish intent, and instead become beacons of encouragement and sources of welcome and goodwill to all who pass their way. My conviction is such that I see a time approaching when even the demonic spirits may be converted to the light, undergo transfiguration, and work unceasingly for the healing of the whole created order. It is my deepest desire to show the common run of humanity that it too can enter the realm of mystical enlightenment if only it will leave self behind, and follow in trust and humility the way of the saints, who gave up their lives with passionate ardour for the service of their contemporaries. We thought in Chapter 12 about the 'rich young man' who could not sacrifice his material resources in his quest for eternal life. Indeed as separate individuals such a renunci-ation is all but impossible. It is only when we pass beyond the barrier of separation to the world of composite unity that we can give up mundane advantages without demur, indeed without even being aware of the sacrifice. Therefore the right way forward of the seeker after eternal life is 'mucking in' with the workers who clean the streets, mine the earth, man the fire brigade, guard the common order in the police force, and tend the dangerously injured in the paramedical crews that operate the ambulances. This is only a sample of the unnamed multitude of heroes on whom our common life depends. When they do their work, away from squabbles about payment and other mundane concerns, their efforts assume cosmic importance. Did not Christ tell us that anything one does for any one of his brothers, however insignificant, one does for him (Matthew 25.40)? When they are in the thick of their work, their mundane squabbles pale into insignificance, for there is now a human life to be preserved. And this applies to all of us who render some service to the community. The fireman or the police officer is part of a greater crew or force, and their identity is magnified in this corporate body of servants of humanity. The Son of Man who was also the Son of God said, 'Among you, whoever wants to be great must be your servant, and whoever wants to be first must be the slave of all – just as the Son of Man did not come to be served but to serve, and to give up his life as a ransom for many' (Matthew 20.26–28). If the plutocrat who sought eternal life had been able to sink his life, which was after all his greatest fortune, with the multitude, he would have known at least something of eternal life even then, and as his service increased, so would his love for God's creatures also have grown warm and compelling. He would have lost his small ego self and discovered a far greater identity which would have embraced the whole world.

I truly love William Wordsworth's 'Valedictory Sonnet to the River Duddon'.

I thought of Thee, my partner and my guide,
As being pass'd away. – Vain sympathies!
For, backward, Duddon! as I cast my eyes,
I see what was, and is, and will abide;
Still glides the Stream, and shall for ever glide;
The Form remains, the Function never dies;

While we, the brave, the mighty, and the wise,
We Men, who in our morn of youth defied
The elements, must vanish; – be it so!
Enough, if something from our hands have power
To live, and act, and serve the future hour;
And if, as toward the silent tomb we go,
Through love, through hope, and faith's transcendent dower,
We feel that we are greater than we know.

How right St Paul was when he wrote, 'No wonder we do not lose heart! Though our outward humanity is in decay, yet day by day we are inwardly renewed. Our troubles are slight and short-lived, and their outcome is an eternal glory which far outweighs them, provided our eyes are fixed, not on the things that are seen, but on the things that are unseen; for what is seen as transient, what is unseen is eternal' (2 Corinthians 4.16–18). It is quite true that the superficial person, governed by the ego, that looks for rewards and recompense, is to pass away, but the inner person, the soul, grows by experience, suffering and a transcendent faith that all will be well despite every indication to the contrary. It will come into its own when we die, and we must take care that it is allowed its due of attention now, so that it may build a spiritual body to take with it to the halls of the afterlife where judgement is given according to its capacity to face the divine light and love that confront all who have made the great transition.

In the company of Jesus we are wise to repeat, 'While daylight lasts I must carry out the work of him who sent me; night is coming when no one can work' (John 9.4). The world is the place of our operation, and the means are the present circumstances. It is worth while giving our thanks to the wonders around us, and hope that we may leave the world a better place for our service. I never cease to recall another marvellous sonnet, 'God's Grandeur' by Gerard Manley Hopkins.

The world is charged with the grandeur of God.
It will flame out, like shining from shook foil;
It gathers to a greatness, like the ooze of oil
Crushed. Why do men then now not reck His rod?
Generations have trod, have trod, have trod;
And all is seared with trade; bleared, smeared with toil;

And wears man's smudge and shares man's smell: the soil
Is bare now, nor can foot feel, being shod.

And for all this, nature is never spent;
There lives the dearest freshness deep down things;
And though the last lights off the black West went,
Oh, morning, at the brown brink eastwards, springs –
Because the Holy Ghost over the bent
World broods with warm breast and with ah! bright wings.

What we are, to return to the question that started this chapter, is
who we are. We may be selfish, covetous people intent only on
our own satisfaction, or we may be servants of the world intent
on allaying at least a little of the pain around us; we may be
sadistic torturers intent only on satisfying our lust for revenge on
those who hurt us when we were small and defenceless, or we
may be protectors of all that is beautiful in human nature,
prepared to give up our lives for our universal friends whether
human or animal; we may be destructive agents intent on the
elimination of all that we dislike in our world including other
humans whose race or life-style offends us, or we may be world
teachers and saviours like the Christ and the Buddha. Gautama
was a prince who had to renounce all human priorities before he
could start his great teaching work; the prince became a
mendicant monk. Jesus was a figure of utmost mediocrity in his
home town of Nazareth, so much so that when he visited his
townspeople, they cast scorn on him. After all, he was only the
carpenter's son! And so, from the polarities of princedom and
social obscurity came the two whose lives and work fully
ennobled the human condition. How often did their followers
sully the greatness of their teachers? And yet their work goes on. I
cannot envisage any future prophet or teacher eclipsing the
authority or teaching of either of these two world teachers. But
we desperately need many teachers following in their footsteps to
bring their message to a bewildered world. Any such teacher
must first have conquered themselves, so that they do not strive for
personal honours. This is a very great test of integrity.

The mystic knows that there is a far-off country where we are
all one, not merely in the love of God but in our relationship one

with another in that love. God is spoken of as 'nothing' by the greatest mystics. This confusing word does not mean that there is no God at all, but that God is beyond rational form and description. God can only be known in negative qualities: the cloud of unknowing, the divine darkness, emptiness, not this – not that, beyond good and evil. This last is especially challenging to our moral sense, for it could be read to imply that the supreme reality is amoral. As such the phrase has been used by various antinomian groups to justify their style of living. In fact it means that the greatness of God embraces all antitheses and transcends them. Nicholas of Cusa, a cardinal of the Catholic Church, described God as beyond the coincidence of contradictories. Thus in the divine nature all natural qualities are comprehended and brought into a divine synthesis that is far beyond the dualism of Aristotelian logic, such as we saw in Chapter 12. If one takes, for example, the Parable of the Prodigal Son, neither the returned, forgiven scapegrace nor his outraged, virtuous brother exhibits the whole truth. In the world of God both are to be changed into beings of such light that even their earthly darkness (the lasciviousness of the Prodigal Son and the righteous indignation of his 'good' brother) is swept into the love of God. 'God is light, and in him there is no darkness at all' (1 John 1.5). The reason for this is that all worldly darkness and light have been taken up by the divine nature and changed into the uncreated light that is the great outflowing energy of God which the mystic knows. All that can be said positively about God is in terms of light and love, but of God as being we know nothing. Yet what we do know can give us cause for praise and thanksgiving for ever and ever. It is of note that while any mystic will affirm the negative quality of God and the ineffability of their experience, they cannot stop talking about it. This is because such an influx of love has entered their soul that they cannot cease until everyone has been able to share in their love and joy. It is not surprising that the mystic will see far beyond religious denominations and the barriers set up by the rational mind. The mystic alone can see the wood for the trees. It is not surprising that, at least in the Semitic religions, especially Christianity and Islam, quite a number of them have been executed as heretics.

Judaism, until our own time, has not had the civil authority to kill anyone, but what it organized in the event of Jesus' crucifixion suggests that it could easily partake of the cruelty of its daughter religions. When religious orthodoxy becomes judgemental and fanatical the most heinous crimes can be committed in the name of God.

Fortunately there is a nobler face to humanity than this, the face of Christ. If we follow him in faith and love, we may take inspiration from these words: 'Dear friends, we are now God's children; what we shall be has not been disclosed, but we know that when Christ appears we shall be like him, because we shall see him as he is' (1 John 3.2).

And so a book that starts in the depths of depression ends in the exaltation of the human spirit in God. Maybe the span between these two experiences is less extreme than would appear at first sight: the clue may lie in the human yearning for perfection. The end of the human search is not so much new discoveries, diverting as these may be, but the peace that passes understanding. This is what Jesus promises his disciples in John 14.27: 'Peace is my parting gift to you, my own peace, such as the world cannot give. Set your troubled hearts at rest, and banish your fears.' This peace is something more than a freedom from unrest; it is a mutual sharing in the good things of life, so that we do not have to hide anything from our neighbour, who is the person next to us at any one time, and by extension, the whole human race and indeed the entire created order. We can be at rest in each other's arms, and give unqualified support to anyone who is in need. 'Come for water, all who are thirsty; though you have no money, come, buy grain and eat; come, buy wine and milk, not for money, not for a price' (Isaiah 55.1). One buys by giving freely of oneself in the great quest for wisdom, the great unceasing service to one's fellow creature. There is joy in sharing of oneself with other people and receiving from them their unconditional love. This is the *Shalom* that is the Hebrew equivalent to this outgoing goodwill that finds its fulfilment in loving service to all around us. In this life we come closest to the heaven we glimpse far away when we share in such universal peace. It is the divine presence among us in the present moment.

I saw Eternity the other night
Like a great Ring of pure and endless light,
All calm, as it was bright,
And round beneath it, Time, in hours, days, years
Driven by the spheres,
Like a vast shadow moved, in which the world
And all her train were hurled;
The doting lover in his quaintest strain
Did there complain,
Near him, his lute, his fancy, and his flights,
Wit's sour delights,
With gloves, and knots the silly snares of pleasure
Yet his dear treasure
All scattered lay, while he his eyes did pour
Upon a flower.

So begins Henry Vaughan's masterpiece 'The World'. The illusions of the world pass away but the life eternal illuminates each passing moment with a significance far beyond anything we can see, until we have passed from selfish regard to universal comprehension. It may require a sharp depressive episode to cause us to take this leap into the unknown, and then at last we begin to live like Christ-filled human beings. In our suffering comes our greatest joy, like a woman enduring the pains of parturition to give birth to a splendid infant.